Contents

Contents

SCHOLASTIC

YOU CAN

Crea
OUTI
class

Rosaleen

FOR AGES
3-7

> "Being outdoors had a positive impact on children's levels of creativity"
> *(Dfes)*

Acknowledgements

Author
Rosaleen Joyce

**Development
Editor**
Simret Brar

Editor
Roanne Charles

Assistant Editor
Margaret Eaton

Cover illustration
Punchstock/BrandX

Illustrations
Q2A Media

Series Designer
Catherine Perera

Designer
Q2A Media

Text 2007© Rosaleen Joyce
© 2007 Scholastic Ltd

Designed using Adobe InDesign

Published by Scholastic Ltd
Villiers House
Clarendon Avenue
Leamington Spa
Warwickshire CV32 5PR

www.scholastic.co.uk

Printed by Bell and Bain Ltd.
3 4 5 6 7 8 9   9 0 1 2 3 4 5 6

Mixed Sources
Product group from well-managed
forests and other controlled sources
www.fsc.org   Cert no. TT-COC-002769
© 1996 Forest Stewardship Council

FSC

British Library Cataloguing-in-Publication Data
A catalogue record for this book is available from the British Library.
ISBN 0-439-94559-3
ISBN 978-0439-94559-2

In memory of my dear departed mother and with especial thanks to Pat, Sean and Roisin for their loving support and encouragement.

Introduction

Why do we need to play and learn outside?

Think for a moment about how you feel when you have been for a brisk walk in the fresh air. You feel better, more relaxed and ready for the next task ahead. Children are just the same. Being outside enables them to move more freely, breathe more easily, think more clearly and learn more readily. Play, movement and a range of sensory experiences are essential features of learning for young children.

We live in a culture where it is increasingly difficult for parents and carers, childminders, teachers and practitioners to allow their young children to use the outdoors as a teaching and learning resource. This is a great shame because it limits children's capacity to learn. Where better for them to become aware of risk by taking responsible risks while learning to manage their own safety? And where better to have fun and set challenges? Where better to take meaningful exercise and stay healthy while learning about themselves and their environment? Where better also, to take time to work though and solve basic life problems as they develop skills and confidence for later life? To work with others in different age groups, to collaborate and confer in a vast range of activities, where better to do this than in the great outdoors?

To allay fears about health and safety, educational settings must have clear guidelines about using outdoor spaces, just as they have indoors – for example, 'You must walk in the corridors'. It is essential that a thorough risk assessment is done of the area used and that this is reviewed regularly. If you go further afield – to the park or the woods – go there first with colleagues and undertake a risk assessment. You might find the suggestions in Chapter 7 useful when doing this, along with the photocopiable risk assessment form on page 56.

In addition to all of this, it is now a requirement of all registered settings to include outdoor play in their provision. Government thinking has realised that young people need more than a five- or ten-minute run in the playground each day. To become healthy, broad-based learners, they need frequent access to the outdoors as part of their curriculum across all areas of learning. The environment outdoors offers stimulation with many challenges and opportunities.

It does not matter what type of space you have, its size or accessibility. What is really important is that you understand the relevance and necessity of outdoor play in a young child's life. Can you provide a space for children to dig, plant and grow? Can you harvest their produce and enjoy it together? Is there space for children to run, jump, twirl around? You may say, 'But I only have a small yard and my class is on the first floor.' Even those children can enjoy their small outdoor space if the time is thought through and carefully planned.

As you turn the pages in this book I hope you will begin to understand, or confirm your own belief, that outdoor learning offers so much to our young children.

About this book
This book is designed for all practitioners working with children aged three to seven.

For the purpose of clarity I have used the term 'practitioner' to mean anyone working with three- to seven-year-olds, whether that is a childminder, an after-school club worker, a teacher or a nursery nurse. For the same reason, the term 'setting' covers all provision in the maintained, private, voluntary or independent sectors, whether that is a playgroup in a community centre or a Reception/Year 1 class in a school.

How to use this book
My advice is first to dip into a chapter that interests you and move out from there to other chapters and topics that appeal. If you can find the time, try to follow up some of the book and website references given at the end of some 'Tips, ideas and activities' sections. The more you can learn and widen your own understanding of the subject, the more you will have to offer the children. Try out some of the ideas and activities and jot down the outcomes, including how you feel about working in this way. You can do this in the book itself, particularly if it is your own copy, and use it as a working tool.

You Can... Practise close observation

We need to help children to develop their close observational skills. One way to do this is to use popular play themes outdoors, for example superheroes. This is a useful vehicle for leading the children into looking more carefully at plants, wildlife and their surroundings in a way that will appeal to their imaginations. You might want to introduce some props to support the play theme such as 'power beads' which, once they are put on, will help the children to see everything more clearly.

Thinking points

- The younger the children, the smaller the group should be in order to ensure quality adult interaction with each child and quality interaction with each other. A group of two or three children aged three, and a group of four to six of four- to seven-year-olds would be ideal.

- Once the focused activity is over, give the children time to explore these ideas independently through play.

- Be aware of how much you are talking and how much time you are giving the children to respond and listen to one another's ideas and thoughts. We can all be guilty of spoiling the best-planned lessons by talking too much.

- Are the children appropriately dressed for the weather outside? Even superheroes need to look after themselves and keep warm and dry! A cold or wet child will not be motivated to learn. A shivering adult will not be having much fun either!

Tips, ideas and activities

- Once outside, look all around with your group of children; look at the ground, look at the sky. Ask the children what they can see, hear and smell. Can they find any puddles? How did the puddles get there? Why is there a puddle here and none over there? Will that puddle be there tomorrow? Allow the children to pick up sticks if they wish. Explore grass, plants, weeds and trees in the area. What can the children see?

- Ask the children what happens when you gently touch a plant with a stick. Remind them to look very look closely and treat things carefully. Explain that as superheroes they will be able to see tiny little raindrops on the blades of grass or weeds. Not everyone can see such tiny things. Ask how the raindrops got there. Demonstrate how to catch a raindrop gently on a finger, hold it there and show it to everyone.

- Suggest to the children that they go out with their parents or carers and show them their special powers. Encourage them to show their families how to look really closely and catch a raindrop.

- Show the children in well-defined easy stages how to do up their own zips, put their own wellies on the correct feet and so on. Can the children decide for themselves when they get outside if they need their hoods up or not?

- Let the children help you to search the internet for colouring sheets of their favourite superheroes.

- Create your own 'raindrops' in a puddle outside using pipettes of different sizes – from the smallest medicine dropper to a really big turkey baster. Talk about the beautiful patterns the raindrop makes as it hits the water.

You Can... **Explore written texts outside**

Young children need lots of different opportunities to make marks and to develop their understanding that written texts carry meaning. This can be done very successfully outdoors where children can move as they learn. To make these learning experiences motivating and meaningful, look to base some of the texts used outside on the children's own ideas and suggestions. The texts can be realistic or based on imagination.

Thinking points

● Have you observed the children sufficiently to identify which themes they are following when they play?

● Are you sure you are following ideas that the children enjoy?

● As part of your outdoors continuous provision, do you have areas where children know they will always be able to find big and small mark-making tools as well as fiction and non-fiction books to look at?

● Always be aware of group size. The rule of thumb is to keep this as small as is practicable.

● If you are constantly having to stop because a child is not listening, you might need to reflect on how you are organising the teaching.

● Once a child's attention wanders, look at the source of the distraction. Can you incorporate this into your activity to keep the child on task?

Tips, ideas and activities

● Set the scene by talking about the important jobs that superheroes do: *Superheroes help people. They rescue animals. What other special jobs do they do?* Write down the children's responses.

● You can use the children's ideas to create a golden box of 'mission cards'. These can be typed statements, cut out and stuck on bright holographic card before being laminated.

● Make a circle with the children, standing around the golden box. Hold hands as you sing, to the tune of 'London Bridge is Falling Down':
We are superheroes, heroes, heroes.
We are superheroes. We're here to help you.
Let's look in the box of cards, box of cards, box of cards.
Let's look in the box of cards to see what we can do.

● Invite a child to choose a card, and read it out together. For example: *Please help me. My cat is stuck up in the sycamore tree.* Set your superheroes to the challenge.

● The children may need props to enhance their play. Capes of different colours are an invaluable resource for superhero play. These can simply be pieces of fabric, net curtains, old pillow cases, cot blankets – anything that can have a length of tape attached to either side.

● Encourage the children to write their own mission texts on a large board outside. You could leave blank cards and big felt-tipped pens outside for the same purpose. Ask the children to read their statements to you for you to scribe on the back. These cards could then be laminated and added to the golden box, thus giving value to the children's emergent writing.

● Regularly check your box of outdoor books to ensure they cover the children's current interests.

You Can... **Develop spatial awareness**

We all need to know where we are in relation to other things. There is so much out there in the world for children to explore and understand. We need to teach them how to use all of their senses to help them use their space safely and imaginatively. Using the superhero theme, we can explore relevant ways in which to develop these skills.

Thinking points

● You might have a child in your group who is visually impaired or with another specific disability. You need to consider how that child's needs can be met. Who can you consult? Will the SENCO in your setting be able to advise you?

● Encourage the children to concentrate as they develop their skills and allow others to concentrate too.

● Very young children find it very difficult to wait for what they want, whereas an older child is already developing this skill of delayed gratification. Sometimes we keep our youngest children waiting too long before they can go and choose their special stick or magic stone.

● Try to create different levels in your outdoor space. A bird's-eye view from the top of a tree stump will look very different from a view at ground level.

Tips, ideas and activities

● Superheroes have to move very quickly in a world which has so many jobs for them to do. Teach the children how to transport and store equipment quickly and safely. When they are able to do this on their own, encourage them at tidy-up time to work with another child to transport boxes of equipment, large outdoor construction materials such as bread crates, planks of wood, milk crates and so on.

● Ask the superheroes to fend off a large group of baddies by grabbing a stick or stone from the ground and imbuing it with their own special powers.

● Sticks of all shapes and sizes, are an essential outdoor resource. We can teach children how to handle them safely, no matter the size of the sticks. Children need to know what is happening at both ends of the stick to ensure it isn't touching anyone. If the children understand that they will have to put the stick down if it does touch anyone, they very quickly learn the skills they need to be able to keep hold of their chosen stick. These are the essential lessons of spatial awareness. Prompt children to ask themselves questions such as: *Where am I in relation to the stick? Where is the stick in relation to everyone and everything else?*

● As superheroes, children love throwing stones, and we can teach them to do this safely. This will help them to judge distances between themselves and other objects in space. Let them take turns to throw stones into a bucket of water or a puddle, away from people, buildings, windows, cars and so on.

● Explain to parents and carers why you are teaching children to do these things.

You Can... Use the outdoors to introduce a narrative

Young children need experience of and practice in developing their communication skills. They have much to say and many stories to tell, but they need to learn how to structure these ideas and accommodate other people's points of view. If you can talk through what you are doing and feeling as you introduce a storyline into the play, you are equipping the children with the language and structure they will need to create stories of their own.

Thinking points

● Think about what interests and motivates the children before you begin. You might have a favourite story line that you want to introduce However, try to balance your ideas with those which you observe as the children engage in free play.

● Think carefully about group size and composition. A mixture of ages can be interesting (say, between three and seven years). Try to keep in mind that every member of the group needs to feel they have a voice.

● Are you listening to the children, their ideas and suggestions? Are you listening to them as much as you are expecting them to listen to you?

● Give children plenty of time to think through their ideas.

Tips, ideas and activities

● Cover with some shiny silver material a log or length of blocks which is long enough for all of your group to sit astride. Tell the children to hold tight because your spaceship is ready for lift off. Count down and blast off! Talk through what is happening as you climb higher and higher into the sky. Invite the children to contribute by commenting on what they can see, hear, smell, touch and taste. Talk about how you are feeling: *I've got a dry taste in my mouth. I'm really scared. I've got to hold on really tight in case I fall off.*

● On arrival on a new planet, help each other to disembark. Carefully look and walk around, talking about what you can see. Return to Earth when the children are ready.

● Encourage the children to take turns in conversation and to listen to each other.

● Leave the props outside and on subsequent days join in with the children as they develop their own narrative. Allow them to lead. Don't be tempted to take over and develop the storyline in the way you would like it to go. Remember when sharing the play that by talking through what you are doing and feeling, you can help to develop the language needed for playing cooperatively.

● Share the Jill Murphy story *Whatever Next!* (Macmillan) on your return from space. The young bear in this story wants to go to the moon. Set up an interactive story box outside using the props from the story and the book itself to enable the children to retell this narrative by themselves.

You Can... **Explore outdoor habitats**

The outdoor environment is full of big and small creatures which live in the trees, on plants, under the ground, under log piles, in the compost, everywhere. There is so much to learn about these creatures and their habitats, so much to see and talk about. We need to teach our children how to look after these creatures and their homes since they are a very important part of our world.

Thinking points

● Do you know the names of the birds that most frequently visit your outdoor spaces? Do you know how they build their nests? Could we try and make a nest ourselves?

● Think about organising a workshop where children can make nesting boxes for birds. Perhaps your local countryside rangers could help you with this.

● Do the children understand that all creatures living outside have similar needs to ourselves (food, water, shelter and care)?

● Collect a range of stories and non-fiction texts about different habitats that you can share with the children.

● It might be a good idea to have a copy of the Countryside Code displayed prominently in your setting for children and parents/carers to refer to frequently for awareness of how we can protect our outdoor habitats.

Tips, ideas and activities

● Ask the children to think about the animal that makes those little hills on the playing field. Why and how does it move all that soil to the surface? What does the creature look like? How big is it? Ask the children to draw a picture of what they think the animal looks like. Show them a life-size picture of a mole and make comparisons between their ideas and the picture.

● Invite the children to create representations of various outdoor creatures, using natural materials such as sticks and twigs, stones, berries and leaves. These can then be digitally photographed by the children and shown to everyone back indoors on the interactive whiteboard. Encourage the children to talk through their creations as they are presented.

● Leave these creations outside at the mercy of the elements and revisit them frequently, noticing and talking about changes. This kind of ephemeral art has lots of possibilities for learning and really appeals to children's imaginations.

● Explore a basic food chain by playing the following simple game. Use props for this if you wish, such as a pair of wings for the fly and four pairs of legs for the spider. Ask one child to be the spider looking for the fly (another child), who is busy flying around. The spider can say or sing to the tune of 'Michael hammers with one hammer':

I'm a great big spider, spider, spider.
I'm a great big spider. I'm going to eat you.
The spider catches the fly and eats it.
Along comes a frog who loves eating spiders…

● Repeat with different children taking on the roles.

● Look at the RSPB website (www.rspb.org.uk/birds/guide) for more information about common birds the children might see at home or at school. RSPB Kids (www.rspb.org.uk/youth) will also provide you with games, activities and fact sheets.

You Can... **Explore and create habitats for minibeasts**

Most young children are fascinated by minibeasts. And minibeasts are everywhere in the outdoor area – on the leaves of plants, under stones, in clumps of grass. Many children are frightened of these creatures or do not value their importance and will automatically step on an ant or spider if they see one. We should teach children how to identify, respect and take care of these very important members of our environment.

Thinking points

● Think about how you can deal with any children's fear of minibeasts. Are there any interesting ways in which you can reduce it?

● Are you aware of what types of minibeasts are out there? Do you know how they grow? What do they eat? Where do they live? You will need to be prepared to answer such questions from the children. What resources will you need to help you do this?

● Are the children clear about what they can touch and pick up? It's fine to pick up a worm if it is handled gently and then returned to its home. Are the children aware of the need to look after themselves as well as the creatures? Will they remember to wash their hands after handling creatures and their habitats outside?

Tips, ideas and activities

● A lot of young children will see spiders being flushed down the toilet at home, or worse. Take the time to explore some of these issues with the children as they talk about them.

● Make laminated minibeast identification sheets and give these to the children, with magnifying glasses. Tell the children to go outdoors and see if they can spot any of the minibeasts on their cards.

● You can create your own 'minibeast hotel' in the outside area. This might consist of a pile of logs or sticks of different sizes. As the logs begin to rot down small creatures will begin to move in and you will have your own designer minibeast resource.

● If there is a tree that is too big in your garden or outdoor area, you might consider pollarding or coppicing. Add the dead wood to your log pile to create an invaluable wildlife habitat.

● Your local council garden maintenance team will be able to provide you with small tree stumps which you can place around your outdoor area. These stumps need to be small enough for the children to be able to tilt for themselves to see what is living underneath. You can show the children how to do this safely and how to return the minibeasts' home to its original position once they have finished looking.

● Kneel or bend down with a small group of children and quietly explore what is happening on the ground. Use a small stick to gently turn over leaves and pieces of moss to see what is underneath. Observe the ants scurrying with their heavy or very large burdens. Follow them to see where they are going.

● Share with your children the story of one little minibeast's struggle to grow wings: *The Crunching Munching Caterpillar* by Sheridan Cain and Jack Tickle (Little Tiger Press).

You Can... Teach children how to look after themselves

As well as teaching children the names and features of their environment, it is also our responsibility to teach them how to be safe within that environment. Always keep in mind that we do not want to frighten children, but we do want them to be safe and properly informed so that they can operate independently within their outdoor environments. We also want parents and carers to know that their children are safe while they are enjoying the outdoors and increasing their independence.

Thinking points

● Before talking to the children, think about how they should be able to look after themselves in various places such as the playground, the park and the street.

● What are the potential dangers outside? What do children need to watch out for?

● One of the hardest lessons for young children to learn is that they have to take responsibility for their own actions. This means taking responsibility for their safety too. Think about how to address this issue.

● Young children need to feel safe and secure, so think about how you can increase the children's confidence and skills in being able to look after themselves outside.

● What are your guidelines about talking to strangers? Are colleagues aware of these guidelines? How do you make children aware of this issue without frightening them?

Tips, ideas and activities

● On a trip to the local park, take the children to the pond and discuss the issue of being safe near water. Or, when setting up outdoor resources that involve water, take a few children with you and talk about how to organise these resources safely.

● Invite a local police officer to come and talk to the children about potential dangers of talking to strangers.

● Take the children on a tour around your setting and the outdoor area. Are they aware of the boundaries within your setting? Ask questions such as: *Why is that fence there around the playground? Why do we need to lock the outdoor gate?*

● Take the children on a walk around your local roads and discuss road safety and the Green Cross Code. Watch the Rosie and Jim video *Be Safe Near Water* with the children to reinforce and extend this learning.

● In your outdoor area, set up a reproduction zebra or pelican crossing. You could simply draw chalk lines on the ground, and provide a jacket, hat and stick 'lollipop' for the crossing supervisor. Help the children to act out the routines and rules they need to follow in order to be safe, reinforcing and adding to the lessons learned when walking on local streets. Talk about what happens when there is no crossing patrol person (whether at a crossing or not). Ask: *What do we need to do then?*

● Take the children on a tour of your outdoor area to look closely at what is growing out there, what is safe to touch and what is not safe. For example, the toadstools that have appeared overnight under the rowan tree are fascinating to look at but they might be poisonous.

You Can... Teach children to accept boundaries

Very young children often find it difficult to accept boundaries; at the same time, older children might like to test these boundaries. Whatever the age group, the boundary rules need to be taught consistently and recalled frequently. In considering boundaries, practitioners' first criterion has to be the overall safety of children and adults within the whole group. We can then go on to consider the wider implications of boundaries and sanctions in terms of learning opportunities for all our children and adults.

Thinking points

● Do the children understand the boundary rules for the outside area and what will always happen if they do not accept them?

● Do the children know where they are allowed to play? Do they understand that it is not safe for them to wander off on their own outside?

● Think about how you could introduce boundaries to a new group of children, whatever their age. How can you be sure that everyone has understood? Do you have a simple system in place where you can monitor how individual children respond to these new ideas?

● The boundaries for your setting may have to be modified for a child with specific learning difficulties, who might not be able to follow the same rules as the rest of the group. How are you going to explain this to the other children?

● Can you find a way of involving the children in setting boundaries and sanctions?

Tips, ideas and activities

● Think about developing a sense of belonging within your setting as a way into setting realistic boundaries that can be monitored by children and adults alike.

● When outside, encourage adults to demonstrate excellent interpersonal skills while dealing with children and colleagues – respecting one another's space, ideas and practices. They can then expect the children to treat them and each other with courtesy and respect, both sides accepting boundaries that will benefit the whole group.

● Do not expect an assimilation like this to happen overnight. Young children often have a range of settings and boundaries to accommodate in their lives. They may be looked after by a childminder as well as attending nursery or school. They may spend time with another parent or grandparent a couple of times a week. Each of these situations may well have a different set of boundaries or, more confusingly for the child perhaps, the same boundaries but with very different sanctions. Learn as much as you can about each child's life outside your setting.

● Avoid confrontation. No one wins in this sort of situation, and it is not a helpful context in which to teach a child how to accept boundaries.

● Keep boundary rules short and simple. For example: *If you poke someone with a stick outside, then you have to go inside.* Give the child, say, one warning before the sanction is applied.

● You *must* carry out your sanctions. There can be no compromise on this. Children need to learn to take responsibility for the consequences of their actions. All adults working in a team need to have a consistent and firm approach to this. If the system breaks down, urgent discussion is needed and with it a clear re-stating of the rationale for setting the boundaries and sanctions in the first place.

You Can... Teach children how to access their environments

Children need to know what is available for them to use, wherever they are. They need to know exactly where everything is, inside and outside. They also need to know how much time they have to explore all that is available. To take all this on board, they need to feel safe and secure. They need to know there will always be an adult at hand to support them if they feel lost or unsure of what comes next. Children also want to know that they can change their environment to suit their play needs.

Thinking points

● Is it possible for your children to have uninterrupted continuous access to the outdoors?

● Can you plan for an adult to be outside all the time? Is that outdoor role planned for and valued equally with indoor roles?

● Do the children understand the routines for going outside and coming inside?

● If your outdoor space is timetabled and you have to go out as a group or if it is not immediately accessible from your setting, think about how you can organise this to include independent choice where possible.

● Are the children able to say, for example: *I don't want to go outside/inside. I want to stay here.* There are times when allowing this is impossible, but are there other times when the child is perhaps making a reasonable choice and you could accommodate them without too much difficulty if you were a little more flexible?

Tips, ideas and activities

● Play a follow-the-leader game going from the inside to the outside and back, where each area is introduced to give an overview of both environments. Accompany the journeys with a chant: *We're going past the digging pit, digging pit, digging pit. We're going past the digging pit. There it is.* Everyone should point to the digging pit and so on as you see it or pass it. Give different children the opportunity to lead, and as you follow you can feed in the appropriate names for areas.

● Teach the children the routines they need to follow for accessing both environments. Will they need to put wellies on to go outside? Will they need their coats? Where do they put their wellies when they come in? What do they do if they can't do up their coat?

● Be patient! Some children might need a lot of support when accessing one or both environments. Your patience should be rewarded, however, by children becoming much more independent after a few weeks.

● Consistency is vital. If the expectation is that coats and wellies go on when the children go out in certain weathers, then they must always go on. That way the youngest children, in particular, feel secure in their independence because they know this is what always happens. At a later stage in their independence, you should allow children to adapt the routines as long as they do not undermine the confidence and security of others.

You Can... **Teach environmental responsibility**

In order to be able to take responsibility for their inside and outside environments, children need to be independent users of these environments. They need to feel that the space belongs to them and that they can modify it and care for it to suit their own and their group's needs. As practitioners, we have to give children lots of opportunities to take the initiative. We need to listen, value and act on their environmental suggestions and ideas.

Thinking points

● Emphasise to the children that the environment they are in belongs to them and the adults who are in it and use it, whether this is indoors or outdoors.

● Think about asking the children what resources they would like in the mark-making area outside for the coming week. How would they like these resources organised?

● Are any of your setting's outdoor areas (for example, the bicycle area or play area) in need of improvement? Discuss this with your colleagues.

● Are there any areas outside that are under-used? You could ask staff and the children how these could be made more attractive and useful.

Tips, ideas and activities

● Collect the children's ideas for improvements and display them in a prominent place for visitors to see. Take photographs of areas before and after changes. Let the children see that their ideas matter and that their environment matters, and that they (the children) can effect change for the common good.

● Teach the children where everything belongs, inside and outside. Talk about the responsibility we all have to ensure that everything is returned to its proper place so that everyone can find what they need and that the outdoor environment, particularly, remains relatively undisturbed.

● Encourage parents and carers to develop such skills at home by giving the children meaningful, responsible tasks. For example, tidying their own toys, helping with the washing, sweeping the patio, raking leaves.

● Invite parents and carers to record some of these positive achievements in the form of a few short statements, dated and signed. Add these to the children's records of achievement to give a more holistic view of their skills development.

● When setting up, tidying or playing in the outdoor area, encourage the children to treat all resources, natural or man-made, with respect because they belong to the whole setting community. Go on to explain that everything out there belongs to all of us. It should not be acceptable to see a three-year-old throw a toy on the ground when they have finished playing with it.

● Children also need to take responsibility for the clothing they take outside, whether it belongs to the setting or whether it is their own. If a child takes off a waterproof jacket once it has stopped raining, he/she needs to know that it is his/her responsibility to bring the jacket inside at the end of the session.

You Can... **Teach children how to use the toilet independently**

We need to give importance and time to the teaching and development of skills necessary for children to be confident users of toilet facilities, both inside the setting's rooms and when out and about. If you bear in mind that most of your newly arrived three-year-olds will only have been out of daytime nappies for about a year or less, this might help you to keep things in perspective and appreciate the need for further teaching in this area.

Thinking points

● Everyone is different. We expect children to have varying skills in holding and manipulating a pencil but often we have no such expectations of variety in toileting skills.

● Expect accidents. Children become really engrossed in activities when they start in a new setting and will often leave it too late to make it to the toilet. Remind everyone frequently for the first few weeks.

● Have spare clothes and a space where a child can be changed with dignity.

● A child may be used to using a potty at home rather than the toilet. Children may have specific toileting needs. Meet with the parents or carers before the children start, to make sure you know about individual toileting needs.

● Whenever the toilet is outside the room, or away from the space you are in, consider the need for continued support, even for older children.

Tips, ideas and activities

● Treat the toilet facilities in your setting as a part of your long-term continuous provision. Make arrangements for how the area will be resourced; be aware of what level of adult support will be available and when; consider what skills are needed to teach the children to use the area independently and how you will monitor the development of these skills.

● Teach the children the process of using the toilet. Reinforce this at story time with discrete pictures of a child using the toilet area. Work with the children to put the pictures in sequence. For example: child going into the toilet area, child sitting on the toilet, child pulling chain, child washing hands, child getting a paper towel, child putting paper towel in the bin. Ask: *What do you do first? What do you do next? What do you do after you have been to the toilet?* Demonstrate how to flush the toilet, wash your hands and so on.

● Once the children have been taught how to use the area, observe them regularly and note their varying levels of competence. Review these notes with your team so that children are supported appropriately.

● Where possible, children should be encouraged to go to the toilet when they want to rather than when told to. They need to learn how to become aware of their own body's needs and be able to respond to those needs.

● When planning a trip out to the woods, for example, where there are no toilet facilities, think ahead. There is no harm in a child discreetly doing a wee behind a tree. In case someone urgently needs a poo, take a trowel and toilet paper in your rucksack, so that you can bury it to prevent animals digging it up and prevent anyone else walking or putting hands in it. Take some moist hand wipes too, as a temporary substitute for soap and water.

You Can... # Explore what our bodies need to be healthy

The outdoors is a wonderful place to think about what we need to do to take good care of ourselves. Simply being outside, running and walking or riding about, puts colour in our cheeks and makes us feel good. It is exactly the same for children. Some children will need more coaxing than others to take exercise outside, but if it's fun and you are committed to it too, then they will enjoy it.

Thinking points

● Check that the children are appropriately dressed for outdoor activities. Always have to hand a spare supply of waterproofs, light fleeces, warm trousers and so on.

● Have you made parents and carers aware that the children will be outside in all weathers and need to be dressed accordingly?

● Are you wearing clothes that will enable you to move freely, comfortably and safely?

● How do you involve the child who likes to stand and observe rather than join in and run about? How can you make sure they keep warm and enjoy the lesson?

● Is there an asthmatic child in your group who may need their inhaler before they go outside on a cold winter's day?

● You might want to set up an area in your setting where parents/carers and children can display photographs and artefacts connected with healthy outdoor activities shared by their family at the weekends, on holiday and so on.

Tips, ideas and activities

● Plan a joint picnic with children and their parents and carers, including healthy foods and lots of games. Encourage fathers to be involved as much as possible. We should all be aware of the absence of male role models for many young children in nurseries, playgroups and schools. Ask parents to send their child to the setting with a healthy snack for the picnic.

● Talk to parents and carers about how we want our children to be fit and healthy. You can display in the setting pictures of what a variety of healthy snacks looks like. You can also talk about those foods that are not so healthy because they contain too much salt, fat, sugar and so on. If you take some photographs of the children eating the food brought on the picnic you can display these with captions highlighting the healthy foods.

● Using a current play theme, explore, for instance, what our superheroes need to do to keep healthy. How do they keep themselves fit? Explore a range of activities to develop these ideas. You might want to set up different levels of climbing and jumping tasks, where the children can see the progression and development and move through these activities at their own pace and in their own time.

● A section of *Involving Parents in Their Children's Learning* by Margy Whalley and the Pen Green Centre Team (Paul Chapman Publishing) gives some useful tips on a variety of ways in which you can involve parents and carers in this aspect of learning. The rest of the book makes excellent reading if you want to know more about developing parent partnerships.

You Can... **Teach children to take snacks independently**

Young children know when they are hungry or thirsty. Children who have additional needs in this area will need to be catered for according to their particular requirements, but with careful planning everyone can safely access snacks outside as well as the more usual inside. Too often we tell children what they need rather than allow them to make decisions for themselves. We should, however, equip them with the skills they need to be able to operate independently in this area.

Thinking points

● Think about how you currently organise your snack time. Is it at a specific time each day? Does everyone have snacks at the same time?

● If the answer to both questions above is yes, why is it organised in this way? Is it in the children's interests or is it just easier to organise?

● Are the children able to choose to have their snack outside? Is it safe and practicable for them to do so?

● Are the children able to choose water if they dislike milk? Are they able to refuse a drink or piece of fruit if they don't want it?

● Do you think of this as an area with learning opportunities? Have you thought about the way you organise this time in terms of developing the children's independence skills?

Tips, ideas and activities

● Plan for the snacks or milk/water area as part of your long-term continuous provision of promoting independence skills.

● Teach the children the process they need to follow in this area if they are to become independent users. As they become more confident and competent they can adapt the process – as long as it does not interfere with other children's needs.

● Teach the children how to use the snacks and milk area outside, just as they do inside. Two children could work together to set out the milk cartons and water bottles, matching a name card to each carton. They could also wash the fruit.

● Set up the snack area outside as a picnic place that the children can access independently. Alternatively, set up a role-play tuck shop and teach the children the dialogues they will need to use in order to get their snack from the server behind the counter. For example: *Please can I have...? Thank you.*

● Encourage the children to go to the snack area when they choose, on their own or with friends. They can find their name label, put it in the box, take their carton and fruit and sit down, inside or outside if it is safe to choose. Have a container nearby for the plastic wrapping on the straws, trays for milk cartons and water bottles and a compost container for leftover bits of fruit. Demonstrate that when they finish their milk, they should place the empty carton on the tray.

● Bring out a jug of water and three or four beakers each time you go outside, all year round. Encourage the children to help themselves. They will love pouring from a big jug! Let them know that they can refill the empty jug inside.

● Read the article '"I can do it myself": Encouraging independence in young children' at www.kidsource.com/kidsource/content4/child.independent.html.

You Can... **Explore the three Rs outside**

To become independent learners young children need to take responsibility for themselves and their environment. To be able to do this effectively they need to be taught how to use equipment, such as large hollow wooden blocks. They need to know where such items belong when they are finished with, and how to stack them safely to protect both the blocks and themselves. Once the children learn and begin to use these skills independently they will have ownership of their space. They will feel proud of their achievements through which they are unknowingly learning some basic mathematical, reading and writing concepts.

Thinking points

● Are sufficient resources available to the children outside? Do the children know what to do if they can't find something they need?

● How do you organise resources for different age groups? For instance, photographs as labels on equipment resource boxes might be helpful for pre-readers.

● Think about the huge number of learning opportunities involved in tidying the outdoor area at the end of a session, such as developing mathematical vocabulary and asking questions: *How many more will fit in the box? What does that label say/show?*

● Do the children know how to carry equipment safely?

● Do you leave enough time for tidying-up activities? Too little time often means raised voices and disengaged children.

● Are you out there with the children picking up toys, modelling appropriate behaviour, praising their efforts?

Tips, ideas and activities

● When the children first come into your class or setting, try to allow at least three weeks, if you can, to teach them how to access and tidy resources. Then spend time monitoring the effectiveness of your teaching by observing the children doing these activities independently. If you give enough time to this initial period you will really reap the benefits in all aspects of learning.

● You can use a superhero toy to encourage tidiness. Introduce him to the children: *This is SuperFrog. He has a very important job to do here with us. Every day after we have tidied up at the end of the session, SuperFrog will walk around with Mrs Green to see if everything has been properly tidied.*

● Plan some focused tidying-up activities outside for a small group with one adult.

● A box full of different-coloured superhero capes could also contain a laminated sheet showing photographs of each cape. The children can count the number of capes on the sheet and then match each cape to its photograph. They can tick off each one on the sheet as they drop it in the box.

● Containers at the digging pit can be labelled using words for older children – for example, *trowels, wooden blocks, spirit levels.* You can hold up a trowel and say, *Where does this belong? Can you help me to find the right container?* Encourage the children to respond in words, descriptively, rather than just pointing.

● Together you can explore the written labels using phonic knowledge skills, if appropriate.

You Can... Help children to make their own props

Children need to be able to make connections between different parts of the environment within their indoor and outdoor setting. They should be taught the skills they need to operate independently in each area, inside and outside, thus being more able to make those connections. Before they can begin to make choices about which props they might need for which activity, children must have enough time to play so they can really develop their own themes and ideas.

Thinking points

● Is there always an adult on hand to support children who want to make props in the workstation? Can the children access the support they need, when they need it?

● Do you have systems in place which will tell you at a glance whether that child in the workstation needs help when using scissors or accessing the painting materials?

● Think about planning for regular informal observations of individual children as they use or make props, to ensure they are supported appropriately.

● Think about the children who do not have the confidence to seek out an adult when they need help – for instance, when they are struggling to fix a piece of ribbon to a laser (stick) using sticky tape. Feed into everyday practice the language needed for children to ask for help and stand up for themselves. Then repeat it in role play using the successfully completed prop.

Tip, ideas and activities

● When the children use sticks to represent special lasers outside, you might want to enhance your workstation inside with suitable accompanying materials such as ribbons, string, wool, tinsel and bright long strips of fabric. Ask the children how they can give additional powers to their laser. Show them what is available in the workstation and teach them how to attach their chosen decoration.

● Continue to develop the resources available in the workstation using cardboard tubes of different lengths and widths and any other safe, interesting and adaptable materials. Point out additions to the children and encourage them to create or enhance props to support their play using these new materials.

● You can really make the most of popular play themes outside by having an outdoor workstation box containing, for example, very large paper clips, big rolls of parcel tape, plastic drainpipe tubes of different lengths, balls of string, long grasses, twigs with leaves on, and so on.

● When planning outdoor activities, remember that there is virtually nothing that you do indoors that you can't do outdoors. However, this doesn't just mean taking the painting easel or sand tray outside. Think about taking the opportunity to do things on a much bigger scale.

● Watch the 15-minute video clip on Teachers' TV (www.teachers.tv/video/214) where Sue Durant and Sheila Sage, early years advisers, enthuse about learning outdoors and describe two activities they have planned for a Reception class, simulating a journey to Bear Land and building a shelter for a teddy bear. (Note: Teachers' TV is not just for teachers. It is for all practitioners working with children.)

You Can... Develop children's big muscles

Where better to develop big muscle movements than in the outdoors where you can seek out and plan for resources on a large scale, whether that involves the children climbing on car tyres or swinging from a tree. In an outdoor environment, children will naturally seek out physical challenges at their own level of development. Our role as practitioners is to observe closely, give children time to develop those skills and move them on when they are ready.

Thinking points

● Are there enough challenges in your outdoor environment to suit the developmental needs of all your children with regard to climbing, jumping, swinging and scrambling?

● Observe the children and the sorts of activities they are setting for themselves and each other before you begin to plan for gross motor skill development. Your observations may tell you a lot about the stage that the child has reached.

● Is your environment safe? Will that tree branch withstand a five- or six-year-old swinging on it?

● Are the children appropriately and safely dressed for these activities?

● Have you thought about why you need to develop children's gross motor skills? What are the implications for learning if you don't?

Tips, ideas and activities

● If you already have trees, logs and tree stumps in your outdoor area, make full use of these. Arrange and adapt them to create different levels for climbing, balancing and jumping to meet the differing needs of your group. A low stump that can be accessed easily by a three-year-old new to climbing will be a good starting point. A tree with simple footholds for the more adventurous could be at the other end of the scale.

● Large ready-made climbing frames with ropes and ladders are an excellent resource for developing gross motor skills, particularly for the older children. However, they often need to be fixed in a permanent position and can take up a lot of your outdoor space.

● A rope hanging securely from a sturdy branch with a piece of wood tied to the bottom can make an excellent swing.

● Big buckets filled with water from the outside tap require strong muscles to carry them to the digging pit where water might be needed for building purposes.

● The children can help set out and put away the outdoor resources, carrying large boxes in groups of two or three, or pushing car tyres. These are all valid activities for developing the big muscles in arms, legs and backs.

● Don't be afraid to ask for additional help if you have a child with a physical disability in your group. It is a vital part of your job as a practitioner to provide the best possible learning opportunities for all children. Take a look at *Physical and Co-ordination Difficulties* by Dr Hannah Mortimer (Scholastic). This book provides a lot of information about identifying and supporting needs along with a range of activities, many of which could be adapted for use outdoors.

You Can... **Develop fine motor skills**

Young children need to develop the big muscles in their arms in order to develop and refine the smaller muscles in their hands and fingers. These are the muscles they will need to use to become competent mark makers, writers, picture makers and craftspeople. When you include your outdoor area in your planning, look closely at your provision to ensure that you are offering enough scope to develop these skills. Choose resources that will give the children opportunities to work on a bigger scale than they can inside.

Thinking points

● Do you plan for activities outside which involve using one-handed tools?

● How do you record children's achievements in the outside mark-making or craft area?

● Observe children at play outside to see how they are using their fine motor skills. How can you interact to develop the skills observed?

● Have you noticed whether the majority of boys are more willing to make marks outside rather than inside? Think about the types of resources needed outside to enhance this interest with particular regard to play themes chosen by the children.

● Are you able to give the children the time they need outside to develop these skills? Timetabling restrictions or difficulty in accessing the area can be a problem. What strategies can you put in place to overcome any such difficulties?

Tips, ideas and activities

● Think big when organising outdoor resources. A big blackboard attached to the wall with playground chalks and big blackboard rubbers all provide excellent opportunities for fine motor skill development.

● Magic painting is always popular and a wonderful learning tool for young children. Use big paintbrushes and big jugs for the water. Let the children fill these themselves from the outside tap. Turning the tap on and off is exercising the small muscles in the child's hand and the bigger muscles come into play as the jug begins to fill up and become heavier and heavier. The children can use their magic paint to make marks on flags, playgrounds or walls. You can vary this activity by using big painting rollers and trays.

● If you have willow structures in your area, encourage the children to keep these under control by weaving new shoots back into the main structure. This can be done too, with extra gentle care, with climbing plants on wire fences such as honeysuckle and clematis.

● Use the natural materials found outside to develop mark-making techniques and control. Sticks can be used to make wonderful marks in mud. They are also good for making patterns in water.

● The children could make a rope hanging and have it attached to a tree by a nail. Challenge them to collect long blades of grass and to twist these into circular shapes. Then demonstrate how to tie these circles of grass to the hanging using more lengths of grass. Over time, the children could weave in seasonal flowers, leaves and twigs. The hanging should be left until the end of the season if possible, when the children say goodbye to it as it dies off. A new hanging can be developed during the next season.

You Can... **Explore different ways of moving**

Young children love to move and experiment with ways of travelling. We can help them to develop their skills and ideas by teaching them how to move safely with confidence and imagination. Even if your outdoor space is very small you can still explore different ways of moving with a small group. It is really important that that you join in with the children as they move, modelling how to turn your hop into a skip, your short step into a long stride and so on.

Thinking points

● Provide a clear framework when it comes to behaviour, both inside and outside. In order to become confident in moving freely, children need to feel safe when they tackle new challenges. They also need to develop a strong, trusting sense of community within their setting.

● Try to make sure that all the children really understand how they are expected to behave outdoors. Are your rules simple and clear? Do all the children understand what will happen if they break the rules? Do you always carry out your sanctions?

● If unacceptable behaviour persists, you could have a word with the child's parent or carer to see if together you can come up with a strategy to resolve the problem. Make sure that both the child and the parent understand that it is their *behaviour* that you find difficult, not the child as a person.

Tips, ideas and activities

● Return to your superhero theme outside, and ask the children to imagine being a superhero. Talk about the need to exercise our muscles to make us strong. Ask the children to run without bumping into anyone and stop when they hear a bang on your tambourine.

● Use talk such as the following to instruct and to encourage technique and imagination: *Superheroes run. Superheroes hop. Superheroes jump, crawl. Superheroes sometimes have to crawl through long, narrow tunnels.*

● You might want to enhance this activity with 'lasers' or 'wands'. These can be sticks of different sizes and shapes from different trees in the area or they can be the cardboard tubes from inside kitchen rolls. You can repeat the same instructions as before, joining in with the children, encouraging them to make large sweeping movements as they sweep their laser high up into the air, down to the ground and so on.

● Make sure that all the children understand the need to be safe. If rigidly applied, a simple rule such as 'If you touch anyone with your laser then you have to put it down' will be acceptable to most children.

● Play music to encourage the children to move freely with their 'lasers'. The older children could work in pairs to create a short sequence of rhythmic movements which they could show to the rest of the group.

● To keep the children together and focused when moving from outdoors to indoors or from one activity to another, ask them to move in a certain way (which you should vary often): *We're going to jump up and down all the way to the digging pit.*

● Look at the really useful section on basic movement skills in Marjorie Ouvry's *Exercising Muscles and Minds* (published by the National Children's Bureau).

You Can... **Develop discriminatory listening skills**

Children need to learn how to concentrate in order to focus on one sense. There are often so many distractions that it can be difficult to achieve this. The environment outside offers many sounds to focus on. Circle time brings the children together as a community to home in on developing listening skills. Children need to be aware of which sense they are focusing on and which parts of their body will help them to do this successfully.

Thinking points
● Think about how you are going to organise the children outside for circle time. Do you have an area that you usually use, with a small tree stump or seat for each child to sit on? You might need to bring out chairs, large building blocks or mats.

● The most important aspect of the circle time strategy is that every member of the group has equal importance. During your circle time, is every child heard and given time to speak?

● Try to make sure that each member of the group can make eye contact with everyone else. In this way the focus moves away from the adult leading the group and the children can be encouraged to speak to the whole group.

Tips, ideas and activities
● The younger the children, the smaller the circle should be. A good rule of thumb is to double the age of a child to determine the appropriate maximum number of children in a particular group.

● Either sit down or stand in a circle holding hands. Encourage the children to close their eyes to isolate their sense of hearing. Say: *Listen really carefully with your ears to all the sounds outside.* Invite them to quietly tell the nearest adult what they can hear. Encourage the children to concentrate by prompting: *Can you hear anything else?* To begin with, the children will probably notice only one thing they hear. With practice they will become more focused and begin to discriminate between different 'big sounds'. This is where the teaching of phonics begins.

● While sitting quietly, perhaps with eyes closed, ask the children if they can hear any birds. Share the rhyme 'Listen to the birds' (see photocopiable page 58). Then invite the children to try to whistle or sing like a bird. Ask: *What kind of bird are you?* Gradually build up the children's vocabulary for talking about birds.

● Have outdoor storytelling sessions. These can be as part of circle time or a way of settling the children back together. A music box playing quietly can be the signal that the story is about to begin. This is an excellent way of helping children to tune in to smaller sounds while still surrounded by the bigger sounds. These are all important early reading experiences.

You Can... **Develop language to describe feelings**

The outdoors creates countless opportunities for children to talk about what they can see, hear, touch, smell and taste – and the feelings or emotions derived from these senses. Take advantage of this to enrich circle time experiences for your children. Use what is already around you, but also enhance the environment by planting and developing your area with nature's lessons in mind.

Thinking points

● What kind of question can you ask to encourage talk about feelings? For example: *It's cold, wet and windy. How does that make you feel?* Model some responses to feed in new language: *I'm shivering. I feel bitterly cold. The tip of my nose is freezing.*

● Consider children who may feel nervous about expressing their feelings in a big group. What strategies can you put in place to make them feel secure? Do they know that they can 'pass' if they do not feel confident enough to speak?

● Are the children encouraged to describe how they feel about the wind blowing the leaves off the trees, the flowers dying in winter, new growth in spring and the wonderful warmth of summer?

● Do the children express, for example, their disappointment when it's pouring with rain and they can't go out on a bike ride?

Tips, ideas and activities

● At the end of a walk in the woods, an outing to the park or a trip to the seaside, gather into a circle. Take turns to talk about what you liked most about the event. Go round again, talking about what you didn't like. We live in a world full of positives and negatives and need to articulate our feelings in both areas.

● As you go around the group, the adults can begin to feed in a wider range of vocabulary that everyone can use in talking about feelings.

● You could focus on a different feeling each week, perhaps related to the weather or changes in the environment. Try to base examples on real experiences relevant to the children.

● You might want to bring a recent conflict to circle time and ask everyone how they feel about it. Deal sensitively with this to protect the feelings of those most directly involved. Being outside the classroom might help others to air their views, and this sharing might contribute to a sense of trust and communal responsibility.

● Circle time lends itself to exploring assertiveness. Encourage the children to talk about things that happen to them outside which they do not like, which make them unhappy. Explore how this can be managed. Teach the children words they can use to express their concern. For example: *Stop that. I don't like it/don't want you to do it*. Practise this within the circle. Then explore how it feels to be shouted at. Ask the children to role-play being assertive. Do they need to shout or scream to get what they want or to stop something happening? Explain that if you are in danger and are frightened it is good to use your voice to scream or shout. But is this a useful strategy in communicating with someone who has taken the stick you were playing with?

You Can... **Develop language to describe texture**

The outside world is full of fascinating textures. These can be seen overhead in intricate cloud patterns, felt underfoot on a bumpy stony path, touched on the bark of a tree. We can develop and extend language for describing these wonders of nature and bring this enriched language to outdoor circle times. These do not always have to be large formal circles. Spontaneous small circles can be just as valid.

Thinking points

● What do you and the children understand about texture? Think about the different textures outdoors (both natural and man-made) that you can discuss with the children.

● Think about the language needed to describe different textures and possible dangers in nature; nettles sting, holly and thistle leaves are prickly and hurt if you squeeze them, while the thorns on blackthorn are so long and spiky, they can pierce your skin.

● How can the textures of man-made structures be described? For example: *The outer surface of the metal drainpipe feels smooth and cold.*

● Do the children bring special found things to the circle? You could lead the talk by feeling the object, looking at it closely and describing its texture before passing it around.

Tips, ideas and activities

● When planning or developing your outdoor area, consider the use of different textured surfaces: a grassy playing area, a stony path, a smooth paved area, bark chippings under a tree.

● When out for a walk in a wood or park, ask the children to go and hug a tree. Invite them to stroke the bark on the trunk. Ask: *How does it feel?* Make a circle around or under the tree and share the children's findings. You can extend their descriptions of 'It felt smooth/rough/hard/scratchy' by adding: *Yes, it does feel scratchy and grainy. The bark is peeling here.* Accept, value and repeat words made up by the children.

● Set up a play farm or dinosaur area outside. Invite the children to collect 'food' for the hungry animals. Talk in a small circle about the textures of the foods chosen: rough hard stones, dry shiny leaves and so on.

● Make your own table as in the example below to show what language you and the children already use and how you can extend it.

Area described	Observation of language used by adults and children	Language to extend
mud	dry hard soft wet slippery	squelchy squishy squashy sticky soggy
leaves	soft prickly sharp	hairy rounded smooth spiky furry
paintwork on doors	soft shiny bumpy	grainy rough smooth
grass	soft long short	damp slippery tickly
puddles	wet muddy slippery	shimmering
stone path	hard bumpy lumpy	pebbles knobbly juddery

You Can... **Develop language to describe sensory experiences**

From the day we are born we begin to use our senses to explore the world. We smell, taste, touch, look and feel to discover how things work and what they can do. We make judgements based on these responses. Our senses are our most basic tool for exploring, finding out about and learning to understand our world. We gradually build up a vocabulary to help us talk about these experiences.

Thinking points

- Is there anyone in your group who has particular sensory needs? How can those needs be addressed during circle time?

- If you have a child in your group with delayed speech, try to make sure that the rest of the children respect the child's right to speak even if they can't be fully understood. Try to engage the children in helping you and each other to interpret.

- The same can be said of a child who speaks English as an additional language. Let the child speak in their own language. Celebrate the new and different sounds the language makes. If an interpreter can't be present, invite other children to help translate.

- Try to learn a few basic words in the child's mother tongue to help them feel their language is valued.

Tips, ideas and activities

Smell

- Pick a range of aromatic leaves, name them and pass them around the circle. Ask the children what the leaves smell like. Do they like the smell? Useful plants are lavender, rosemary, thyme, and lemon balm.
- Explore the outdoor smells after a shower of rain or when the grass has been cut. Make a small standing circle holding hands as you close your eyes and take turns to share your responses.

Touch

- Bring examples of textured materials to the circle for the children to feel and talk about. Lead the discussion to feed in the extended language before passing the object on. For example: *This is a beautiful piece of bark from the silver birch tree. It is smooth in parts but other parts are rough and pitted. Some of the bark is peeling.*

Sight

- Bring laminated pictures of wildflowers and weeds common to your outdoor space to your circle – for example, buttercup, daisy, bindweed and dandelion. Ask the children to examine them closely. Play games to learn the plants' names. The children can take turns to hide a wildflower while the other children close their eyes. When they open their eyes they try to guess or remember which flower is missing.

Hearing

- Be really quiet in your outdoor circle. Listen and talk quietly about what you can hear. Ask the children what they can hear if they cover their ears with their hands. Encourage them to listen to the sound of their own breathing and then a friend's breathing. Are they breathing differently?

Taste

- Have an outdoor picnic during circle time. Ask the children to describe the tastes, smells and textures of the different foods they try. Also encourage them to describe the foods in terms of what they look like. (Make sure all the foods are safe and acceptable for everyone to eat.)

You Can... **Promote a keen interest in nature**

Nature is full of the most wonderful surprises and extraordinary experiences. We can teach children to use all of their senses and whole bodies to appreciate these wonders. In order to enjoy nature we need to stop, look, listen, feel, smell and even taste. Give the children time to share their feelings about what they are seeing, feeling, touching, tasting or smelling. Give them time and opportunity to be inspired by what they experience. Give yourself time to listen carefully to their responses.

Thinking points

● How often do you really stop and pay attention when a child draws your attention to something? Is there a way of keeping tabs on who you listen to most? Is anyone getting forgotten?

● Think about the different resources you already have and those you might need to source to enable the children to explore nature, such as magnifying glasses and binoculars. Items like these could be hung around a child's neck, leaving both hands free to touch and explore.

● What is your idea of what nature is? What are the children's ideas? Think about why nature is important and why we need to take an interest in it.

Tips, ideas and activities

● Talk about the wonders of nettles and dock leaves. Why is it that if you get stung by a nettle there is always a dock leaf nearby? Thoughts like this can be shared at circle time as you give the children information about the world around them.

● Help the children to take digital photographs of items of great interest they see outside. The prints could be laminated and brought to circle time. Talk about the item's special beauty or quality with the group.

● See the beauty of the patterns in a frosty puddle. Gather a small group in a circle, squat down and look closely. Trace the patterns with your finger. Ask questions and make observations. For example: *How did it get here? It wasn't here yesterday. Why is it so cold?* Listen carefully to the children's responses and encourage them to listen to one another.

● On a fairly windy day, ask the children to lie down on the grass and watch the cloud patterns moving across the sky. Do the cloud 'pictures' remind the children of anything? Ask them if they know what is making the clouds move so fast. What are the clouds made from?

● When it is snowing, encourage the children to make footprints and compare the different sizes and sole patterns. Pose questions such as: *Where does snow come from? What does it feel like to touch? At what time of year does it snow?*

● You might be interested in looking at the Swedish Skogsmulle Foundation's website (www.skogsmullestiftelsen.org) to see how learning about nature is introduced through characters who explain how it needs to be looked after, what lives there and so on.

You Can... **Celebrate skills learned**

As adults, when we do something well we love to be praised. So do children. We can encourage them to continue to develop their skills by acknowledging their successes. These can be big or small achievements; they are all important. Each achievement will be relevant to the individual child's stage of development and that is what matters. In drawing attention to these small steps we can give confidence to less able and physically challenged children.

Thinking points

● Not every child will want to be singled out for praise in front of the whole group. Try to find ways to accommodate this child's needs. You might, for example, be able to combine their achievements with those of another child.

● Make sure you aren't praising the same children all the time. Other children will notice this and can become really despondent.

● You may have a three-year-old who always says, 'What about me?' when you are praising someone else or choosing someone to do a task. Try to have this child sitting near you so that you can support them as they listen. Maybe that child could help you sometimes in the circle by holding your keys or looking after your pen.

Tips, ideas and activities

● Think clearly about which achievements you want to draw everyone's attention to. As well as writing or reading skills, focus on practical, physical and observational skills. These can then be applied to outdoor play. Try to select a wide variety of activities across the curriculum and give equal value to all of them.

● Respond to opportunities for small circle time when they arise naturally. Out in the woods or the garden a child might notice the first leaves of spring, for example. Gather a few children from nearby and form a small circle so that the child can share their discovery. This is an excellent chance to praise, celebrate and further encourage close observational skills, and this praise could be shared with the child's parent or carer at the end of the day.

● At the end of an outdoor session, organise the children in a large circle on mats, blocks or tree stumps. Go around the group with each child in turn looking at the person next to them and then telling everyone about something special they have seen that person do outside. When the children understand this routine, you can move on to having the children talk about what particular task the person next to them is really good at. In an activity like this the children will show you what they value as important. It may be very different from your own ideas, but you need to take their views seriously and take them on board because this is how they see the world. They might say, for example: *Janita is really good at climbing trees* or *Paul is really good at helping me to turn off the outside water tap when I can't do it by myself.*

You Can... Share significant outdoor experiences

Circle time offers the opportunity for everyone to speak if they choose. It also tells the practitioner a great deal about the child's level of speech development, listening skills, ability to take turns in conversation and follow a prescribed pattern. Because the outdoor environment is so stimulating and constantly changing, there are always numerous topics worthy of bringing to the whole group – whether this is talk about seeing something special on a walk, or being able to balance on a fallen log in the garden.

Thinking points

● Tell the children that you will gather at a certain time each week to talk about special things they have seen or done outside. These special things can happen at home as well as in the setting.

● Are parents/carers aware of this weekly circle time event? If not, inform them so they can help the children remember particular events.

● Think about recent specific happenings or outdoor events within your setting, jog the children's memories and invite the children to recall these at circle time.

● Think about why it is important for the children to share outdoor experiences. For example, promoting a sense of belonging in a group and a sense of team work, sharing a common understanding, developing an awareness that each child may have a different view of a shared outdoor experience, and so on. What are the advantages and benefits? Discuss these with the children and make sure your staff understand the importance too.

● Tell the children how important it is that everyone can hear their voice. Are they aware of how quiet/loud their voice is?

● Is there a very quiet child in your group who would benefit from sitting beside an adult who can support and prompt as appropriate?

Tips, ideas and activities

● When out on a walk (maybe your weekly walk to the woods), take the children down a path that is surrounded by nettles. (Make sure they are all wearing protective waterproofs and wellies.) Show them how to hold their arms up so they won't be stung. Encourage them to warn their classmates behind of the danger ahead by shouting, 'Nettle alert! Nettle alert!' This sort of controlled, risky activity really appeals to young children and will motivate them to later recall the experience with great enthusiasm at circle time.

● The children could take turns in the circle to recall a shared event in a sequence of single sentences.

● Listen carefully to what the children have to say about outdoor activities, significant changes they have observed, or events that have happened when playing outside at the weekend. You can develop their speaking skills by repeating what they have just said while at the same time modelling the correct grammatical structures, tenses and extended vocabulary. Give the children lots of opportunities to explore the range of sounds and volume their voices can make outside. If there are no serious restrictions regarding noise then let them shout, scream sometimes, sing and whistle.

You Can... Use the outdoors to explore differences

Young children are assailed by many different views and interpretations of the world. It is very difficult for children to accommodate and make sense of them all. We can help them relate often abstract ideas to their own experiences of the world by presenting these ideas in a practical way. Play gives children time to reflect and organise their thoughts and start to make sense of their world and its different cultures and belief systems.

Thinking points

● Your views might not be the same as those heard and expressed in a child's home. Try to make sure that the child in no way feels compromised by this difference. It might be worth talking to parents and carers individually if a potential conflict arises. It is often best to keep discussions at a professional level and concentrate on what the government directives prescribe for all young children, rather than getting bogged down with personal viewpoints.

● Have a close look at your resources. Do they reflect the variety of cultures in your setting/ school/local community? Are your resources a true reflection of the cultures they are aiming to represent? Are the images modern?

Tips, ideas and activities

● Tell the children you are all travelling into space as you have been invited to a meal with the aliens who live behind the silver screen. Consider: *What will they give us to eat?* Talk about the need to accept that different people eat different things. *How will we accept the aliens' hospitality even though we might not like the food or drink they offer us? Maybe we can taste a little and say, 'Thank you, that was delicious'.* Talk about how the aliens would feel if you said, *'Ugh! That was disgusting.'*

● Organise an exotic fruit party outside where the children try lots of different fruits. Encourage them to describe the taste and say whether they like it.

● When learning about festivals such as Divali, Chinese New Year, Eid, Easter and Christmas, it is useful to base the discussion on themes common to all of the celebrations: people send cards; they get new clothes; they visit a special place to pray; they eat special food; they visit family and friends and give presents. Children can relate new information about other cultures and beliefs to their own knowledge of festivals.

● Celebrate the differences that present themselves within your group: skin colour, eye colour and so on.

● Have a look at the NIPPA website (www.nippa.org). This early years organisation in Northern Ireland provides information and training for parents, childcare providers and local authorities.

You Can... Re-enact the story of Noah's ark

In RE, children as young as three start to learn about their own and other cultures and beliefs. The values that underpin this area of learning are cross-curricular and apply to everything we do as practitioners. They involve sharing; taking turns; caring for ourselves, each other and our environments; as well as listening to and valuing one another's viewpoints. All of these are necessary qualities to develop in order to become active members of our group or community.

Thinking points

● Do you know the story of Noah's ark? Familiarise yourself with it before revealing it to the children.

● Do the children know the sequence of events in the story? Do they know which religion the story comes from?

● What is the message of the story? What values does it convey?

● Do the children like the story? Ask them to consider one another's viewpoints about it.

● Do the children know stories that are similar to that of Noah's ark or that convey a similar message?

Tips, ideas and activities

● After a heavy shower of rain, find a big puddle. Use large toy animals, a wooden or plastic boat, a length of wood or plastic to act as a ramp to cross the puddle to the boat, and a figure to represent Noah.

● Tell the children the story of Noah's ark using your props. Let them line up the animals in pairs of varying combinations and take turns to lead them up the ramp onto the boat. Let them choose which animal goes with which, and prompt them to talk about their choices.

● Sing, or chant:
The animals came in two by two. Hurrah! Hurrah!
The animals came in two by two. Hurrah! Hurrah!
The animals came in two by two,
The elephant and the kangaroo,
And they all went marching
On to the ark, to get out of the rain.
Continue the next verse with the next pair of animals.

● Set up a sturdy plank across the puddle to a couple of bread crates or a wooden pallet representing the ark. Let the children sing or chant the rhyme, taking the animals themselves.

● Use percussion to represent the sounds the animals make. Use natural materials such as sticks, stones, bark and so on. The children can play their instruments as they move towards the ark, getting louder as the animals fearfully walk along the plank and becoming quiet as Noah greets and calms them.

● Help the children to role-play the story. Let them take it in turns to be Noah and the different animals. They could rehearse this role play and act it out for parents and carers.

● Seize the opportunity whenever you are near water to talk about the need to look after each other and how to be safe.

You Can... Re-enact the story of Rama and Sita

Children need to learn about the world around them and the people who inhabit their world. The rich variety of cultures and beliefs in our society is often reflected in the vast range of stories attached to those cultures. Children love the inherent drama in these stories; the strong, clear messages such as the triumph of good over evil, light over darkness, as in the story of Rama and Sita. This epic tale lends itself particularly well to the outdoors.

Thinking points

● What activities do you carry out that focus on the beliefs and practices of different cultures? Is there a balance?

● What do your staff understand about other cultures? They need to be well informed in preparation for any questions from the children. How can you address any lack of understanding or knowledge in you and your colleagues?

● Establish the children's understanding of what another culture, belief or practice is. Think about how to explain these concepts to them.

● Is your setting made up of children from different cultures? If so, this could be an interesting talking point at circle time. If not, how can you inform the children of the existence of other cultures, beliefs and practices?

● Children need time to think about new learning. This also applies when they are introduced to a new way of thinking or set of beliefs. Do the children have time and space to absorb new ideas?

Tips, ideas and activities

● Tell the story of Rama and Sita (ideally at Divali time) under a tree in the garden, wood or park, then act it out. Keep the storyline simple to make it easy to re-enact. See the photocopiable example on page 54.

● Provide some props for the monkeys who helped Rama to find Sita – perhaps a mask or a pinned-on tail. Rama might like to wear a crown and Sita a shimmery gold or red shawl.

● Make a collection of mud diva lamps. Show the children how to mould a ball of mud into a small pot. Decorate the exterior using natural materials found nearby, such as leaves, twigs or small shiny stones. Leave the pots to dry in a sheltered space, then place a tea light in each and use the divas to line a wide pathway. Act out the story of Rama and Sita returning home, their pathway lit by beautiful divas. Make sure the children are completely safe when the divas are lit. Explain the dangers of fire and ensure that as the children walk along the path the divas are not near them or their clothing.

● Children often reject one another in their free play. Explore these feelings at circle time and draw parallels with the story. You can ask: *How do you think Rama felt when his dad sent him away?* Relate it to their own experience by asking: *How would you feel if you wanted to play a game of superheroes with your friends or family and they all said, 'Go away! We don't want you here'?*

● Discuss the story of Rama and Sita with the children. What do they like or dislike about it? What do they understand about where the story has come from and what it means?

You Can... Create an outdoor market for Eid

As children's experience of the world grows they will notice the differences and similarities in people. Learning about different festivals is a great way to open children's eyes to cultures and beliefs and the people that follow them. This activity explores festivals through a focus on Eid and stresses the idea of difference as a positive thing.

Thinking points

● Are you aware of the basic principles of the cultures and beliefs you are teaching? For example, how is your knowledge of Ramadan?

● Do you have Islamic symbols or artefacts that you could show the children? Do you know exactly what the artefacts represent?

● Do you know how religious artefacts should be handled? For example, the Qu'ran should always be treated with clean hands and great respect whether you are a Muslim or not.

● How much do you know about the festival of Eid? Think about how you can explore the festival and celebrate it with the children.

● How will you respond if a child makes a prejudicial comment? Think about how you can introduce the idea of equality and of treating other people's beliefs and opinions with respect and tolerance.

Tips, ideas and activities

● As Eid-ul-Fitr approaches, talk to the children about the festival and how families celebrate by cooking special food, visiting one another, wearing new clothes and so on. Tell the children that you are going to celebrate Eid outside by creating a special outdoor market, just like the ones in places where Islam is the main religion.

● Set up a couple of tables outside to represent an outdoor market selling Eid products. Drape the tables in brightly coloured saris to give a festive atmosphere. The children can shop using plastic coins.

● Set up a food stall, selling fruit, vegetable samosas, and naan breads. Buy traditional Asian sweets, show these to the children and put them out on the market stall. Children could also try making saltdough sweets to add to the produce on display.

● Add a clothes stall using costumes from your setting. The children could pretend to buy and sell these. Your dressing-up box for the outdoors could include some of the following traditional clothing items: a shalwar kameez, headscarfs, skull caps and so on.

● Set up a toy stall using the setting's props. Children could pretend to be parents looking to buy Eid presents for their children.

● Run a mendhi stall. Show some examples of mendhi patterns and explain that many women and children have their hands decorated with mendhi at this festive time. Make simple mendhi patterns on the children's hands.

● Make enlarged copies of a range of simple mendhi patterns and peg these onto a board for the children to colour in with large felt-tipped pens or playground chalks.

● Laminate a book of photographs of your children running their Eid market stall. Include this in your outdoor festival resource box to encourage recall of the event and stimulate discussion.

You Can... Celebrate the festival of Tu B'Shevat

You can create many learning opportunities when you focus on a festival. For young children it is especially useful because you can concentrate on what people actually do at the festival and repeat those concrete activities, making the experience lively, interesting and multi-sensory. This will help the children to understand that the things people do at a festival often have an underlying meaning, which explains the true purpose of the festival. Lighting divas is a good example of this, signifying the triumph of truth.

Thinking points

● Are you familiar with this Jewish festival? Where can you find out more about it? How can you share this information with your team and with parents and carers?

● Think about strategies that enable children to develop questioning skills. They need to be able to ask questions that deepen their understanding and help them to reflect on the learning.

● How can you model the sorts of questions/thoughts children will need? For example: *I wonder why people want to do that. I wonder what I will remember about this festival.*

● Questions can help children to see similarities and differences. They can remain strong in their own commitments while respecting other people's point of view.

● Be particularly sensitive to children who might be part of a minority group. Try to ensure that they feel secure as these questions are explored.

Tips, ideas and activities

● Celebrate Tu B'Shevat in your outdoor area. Explain to the children that the festival is one of the four Jewish new years (Rosh Hashanahs). It is the 'new year for trees'. Talk about how the festival is a time to celebrate trees and the fruit that grows on trees. Jewish people eat lots of fruit on this day.

● Prepare and then share outside with the children a large salad of fruits that grow on trees, such as apples, oranges, plums, cherries and so on.

● At this festival Jewish people try to eat a new fruit that they have not tasted before. Share some more unusual fruits, particularly those associated with Israel, such as pomegranates, pitted olives and dates.

● Outdoors, teach the children the names of different parts of a tree: trunk, bark, branch, twig, leaf and so on, and the parts of fruits, such as skin/peel, seed/pip/stone and flesh.

● Show and teach the children the names of some of the trees that grow in your immediate area and beyond. Help them to recognise different trees by, for example, leaf shape and whether or not the tree is deciduous.

● Children can use small twigs and sticks to make the first letter of their name. Help them to stick these on small squares of card and make a display.

● Organise a festival to celebrate being outdoors. Invite parents and carers. Remind everyone to dress appropriately for being outside. Share some food after you have explored together the wonders of your outdoor space.

● Suggest to the parents and carers that when they next go shopping with their children they look at the more unusual fruits for sale in the greengrocers, supermarket or farmers' market.

You Can... **Celebrate Chinese New Year**

Babies delight in making patterns in spilt food with their fingers. As soon as they are able to pick up a tool, be it a spoon or a stick, children will make marks. Over time, we are able to distinguish between those marks and give them meaning, whichever culture we are from. Our job is to foster those early mark-making skills until the child learns to write. It is also important that we impart the knowledge that all written languages convey meaning and are of equal value.

Thinking points

● Do you have a range of big mark-making tools in your outside area?

● Can the children make marks in their own language (if it is not English)?

● Allow young children the freedom to hold the tool in the grip of their choice. Insisting too early on the perfect grip can deter a child from experimentation. The pincer grip required for holding a pencil requires highly developed small muscle control.

● Are there language scripts other than English in your setting? For example, welcome signs in all the languages used in your immediate community. If the only language spoken is English, it is even more important that you display other languages to demonstrate to staff, children and families that we are part of a global community.

Tips, ideas and activities

● As part of your celebration of Chinese New Year, look at the written Chinese characters which represent the greeting 'Happy New Year'. Trace them with your finger.

● Make and laminate bold cards showing the greeting. Peg these to a board or fence or stick them on the outdoor blackboard. Encourage the children to trace over the letters with a big damp paintbrush. See if they can reproduce the same marks themselves alongside the card.

● In your outdoor area set up a Chinese stall selling different Chinese artefacts with Chinese numerals and letters on them. Ask two children to be the shopkeepers, and encourage the others to buy what they like from the stall using plastic money. Then ask them to copy the Chinese markings from the artefacts they have bought.

● Ask the children to make 'Happy New Year' markings outdoors in sand, mud and on the outdoor blackboard using sticks and other mark-making tools.

● Help the children to perform a Chinese New Year dragon dance. Mark out a giant Chinese symbol on the ground with paint or chalk and ask the dragon to dance along it.

● Set up a display on your parents/carers' board to inform families about whichever festival you are celebrating. Include, in this case, the story of Chinese New Year which tells how it came about that each year has the name of a particular animal.

You Can... **Explore natural features**

When children are learning any new skill, they also learn the vocabulary they will need to talk about it, describe what they are doing and how they are doing it. It is just the same for learning about the environment outside. In order to make sense of it and engage in discussion about its features, children need the relevant words. In your teaching, give children the real, specific words rather than general vocabulary. For instance, why say, 'That's a tree', when we can say more accurately, 'That's a beech tree'?

Thinking points

● Are you able to name all the natural features of your outdoor area? If not, how can you find out what you need to know?

● Explore the importance of looking at your outdoor area from different levels and different angles (for example, from an adult's height and then a child's height). What are the differences?

● Is there anything you need to change in your environment to create more meaningful opportunities for learning? Will the children be safe as they explore?

Tips, ideas and activities

● Invite a Countryside Ranger to walk around your outdoor area with you and your group, looking at the natural features of the place, naming them and talking about their properties.

● Tree names on laminated cards or other permanent signs can be attached to or stuck under trees in your immediate outdoor area. This will ensure that all adults can correctly identify them all year round.

● Show the children the leaves of three trees from your outdoor area. Talk about how they grow on the stem, what pattern they form. Laminate the leaves and play the following game to reinforce the children's knowledge of the name of each tree and some of its features. Sit the children down and, with their guidance, peg the laminated card on the appropriate tree. Then ask the children to close their eyes. Remove one of the cards. Tell the children to open their eyes, and ask: *Which leaf is missing?* The children can give one another clues such as, *It's the tree with the wavy edge on its leaf.* (The oak.) Continue until all the cards have been removed.

● Have a good range of reference books in your outdoor reading area to enable children and adults to identify birds, leaves, butterflies, minibeasts and wildflowers.

● Before you go out with the children to the garden, woods or the park, sing the song 'What will we see in the woods today?' on photocopiable page 58 to focus their attention on what to look for. On their return to the setting, sing the song again to recall new vocabulary, features and experiences.

● The children can learn more about squirrels as they sing 'The squirrel song' on photocopiable page 58.

You Can... **Examine man-made features**

Man-made urban and rural features are an integral part of the environment and a wonderful source of learning and exploration. Again, children need to be aware of the features and appropriate vocabulary needed to talk about and describe these. We can extend the use of the local built environment to history and geography learning. Any attempts to promote learning outdoors, whatever the subject area, particularly for our three- to seven-year-olds, is to be applauded since this active approach to learning will go a long way to meet their developmental needs.

Thinking points

● Explore your immediate outdoor area for man-made features. Look at the garden. Make a list of everything that has been made or shaped by humans.

● Think about the materials and techniques used to create these structures and objects.

● Look at any man-made structures created using natural materials. Why are they built? What are they used for?

● Think about significant features in your local street, village, town or city. What is the purpose of these structures? Can you visit them? How were they made?

● Generating awareness of the immediate and local environments will help to promote a sense of identity and purpose in your children.

Tips, ideas and activities

● Take digital photographs of the main features in your local street – for example, the church, post office, a bench, a pedestrian crossing. Show these to the children on the interactive whiteboard as part of your preparation for a walk along the street. Talk about the purpose of each feature, and what it looks like.

● Use this activity to teach positional language such as *in front of, behind, beside.*

● Make a sequence of the planned walk, using the pictures as cues: *We are going to walk past the church, along the pavement, over the zebra crossing.*

● Laminate the pictures and use them to recall the walk. Ask the children: *What did we do first? Where did we go next?* Peg the pictures on the fence to encourage the children, in their own outdoor play time, to sequence and reflect on the walk and the learning that took place.

● Set up a simple cold frame (a wooden box with a transparent lid which protects young and tender plants and seedlings) in your outdoor area and use it to grow seedlings in pots. Use Perspex or plastic rather than glass for the lid. Talk to the children about its structure, what it is made of and what its use is.

● Explore different greenhouses. Perhaps you have one in your outdoor area or there is a big one in the local park. Discuss their purpose and construction.

● Make up songs to familiar tunes to reinforce names, features and functions of man-made structures in our environment.

● Contact a local or national geographical or historical association. They can be a valuable source of resources.

You Can... **Teach children how to look after their environment**

When teaching children about the features and functions of different parts of their natural and built environment, we need to remind them of their responsibility for their surroundings. They will often consider this to be a task attributed to adults only because they do not understand the part they can play in developing this role. Sadly, nearly every time we go outside we can talk about the impact of litter, vandalism and graffiti on our lives because they are a constant feature. The children should learn that these do not have to be permanent features.

Thinking points
- What kind of safety rules do you have in your setting regarding picking up litter? For example, children should never pick up glass, needles and other dangerous items.

- Consider investing in a set of litter pickers. They are excellent for developing hand-eye coordination as well as ensuring that the children do not touch dirty rubbish.

- If your outdoor area is repeatedly being vandalised, try to consider ways that you can involve the children and their families to address this.

- Have you discussed issues like graffiti, vandalism and litter with the children? How can you explain these issues? For example, think about the implications of what you are saying when you give the children a set of big playground chalks with the message that they can draw anywhere they like…

Tips, ideas and activities
- Introduce new vocabulary such as *litter*, *vandalism* and *graffiti* when out on a walk with the children.

- Go on a litter pick with the children, ensuring that everyone understands the safety rules. Ask the children to work in pairs, one using a litter picker, the other holding open a carrier bag. After a while they can swap over.

- Draw attention to natural litter and talk about how nature disposes of waste. Can that waste matter be used in the compost bin or to make leaf mould (collected autumn leaves left to rot down, for use as mulch)?

- When drawing with chalks on the playground, talk to the children about the temporary impact of their marks. The next shower of rain will wash the marks away, so they are not permanently affecting the environment.

- Compare the children's chalk marks with spray-paint graffiti on walls and buildings. Ask questions such as: *How does it look? Does it improve the building? Did whoever made the marks have the right to do so? Is it their building?*

- Explore the impact of our behaviour on our environment and the responsibility we have towards caring for the environment. For example, draw the children's attention to any trees that have been damaged by people, and ask them what the consequences of such actions might be. Talk about treating the trees with care, respecting their right to grow and flourish so that everyone can enjoy them.

You Can... **Teach children how to save water**

Children tend not to question the source of natural or man-made materials. Younger children will probably not be aware of where our water comes from before it reaches the tap, or where the sand in the digging pit originated. They often assume there are unlimited amounts of water and sand and so on. We can begin to teach children that these materials are limited, without becoming too technical. We can also teach them about the need to look after these precious resources.

Thinking points

● Wherever children have access to water outside, ensure that the area is safe. You might consider putting bark chippings on grassy areas near a water source to prevent the area becoming muddy and slippery.

● Do the children know how to be safe near water? Are there strict sanctions for those who do not observe the safety rules?

● Does your setting have an outside water tap? One can be installed relatively cheaply and means the children have permanent access to water as a resource to enhance their play.

● Are the children properly dressed when they play with and around water? A pair of wellies and a set of waterproofs means they can explore, fill and spill as much as they like without becoming wet, cold and uncomfortable.

● Think about how you can advise parents and carers about the importance of saving the Earth's natural resources.

Tips, ideas and activities

● Before the children go near water, whether it is to wash their hands or fill a container, teach them how to use it with care. Show them how to turn the tap on and off and encourage them to ask for help if they cannot do this by themselves. Discourage water wastage and stress that water is a precious resource.

● Teach the children how to transport water safely, pour it without spilling and so on. Monitor and support these skills as they develop.

● Rather than pour water down the drain when you have finished washing dolls, for example, put the 'waste' water on the garden or on plants in tubs.

● Show the children how to recycle water. Use rainwater collected in the cover of the digging pit to water plant containers. Set up a water butt to collect rainwater.

● Tie plastic drainpipes to your climbing frame or fence to replicate guttering on the roof of your setting. Put bowls under the down-pipes at ground level. Pour the water collected back down the pipes and act out the rhyme, 'Incy Wincy Spider' as you do this.

● Have a look at the WaterAid website (www.wateraid.org.uk/uk/learn_zone/teachers) to access resources on global communities and water. Learn about the lives of young children from different countries around the world and find out about some of the issues they have to deal with. WaterAid's Key Stage 1 *Water Splash Early Years Teaching Pack* can be downloaded free and is recommended by the National Day Nurseries Association. Informative early years posters are also available.

You Can... **Explore conditions necessary for growth**

The outdoors is the perfect place to teach children about the growth of plants and animals. It is important to keep this teaching quite simple so that the same messages are clearly and frequently observed and experienced by the children. Concentrate on light, food and water – remembering, of course, that not all animals need light for healthy growth. The mole, for instance, manages quite well in total darkness beneath the ground!

Thinking points

● Do the children have a space where they can plant seeds and bulbs, and a wild area as well where they can observe animals and birds? These do not need to be big spaces: small containers, old buckets with holes in the bottom and car tyres are just a few possibilities.

● Do you know about the types of conditions needed for the healthy growth of plants and animals? How much do the children know? Find out what these conditions are and discuss them with the children.

● Think about interesting ways of talking to the children about growth in plants and animals. What kind of examples can you show them?

● Do you have enough appropriate tools for working in the outdoor area safely? The tools must work well and be easily manipulated by the children. Choose lightweight adult-sized trowels and real garden rakes with plastic tines and the handle cut down to a manageable length for young children.

Tips, ideas and activities

● Plant, nurture and harvest foods such as herbs and potatoes, as well as a range of flowers, in your outdoor area. Remind the children about the need to save water, and plant drought-tolerant plants like geraniums and stonecrop.

● Talk to the children about what a plant needs to be healthy. Plant some seedlings in a dark corner of the garden where they will get hardly any light or rainwater. Do they grow as well as the plants in the open?

● Dig up a growing potato or plant and look at the roots. Explain how the plant gets its food (nutrients) from the soil through the roots.

● Place a small log on the grass to use as a seat. After a few days, look underneath. Why is the grass all yellow? Also talk about any minibeasts that live under there. Where do they get their food from?

● Organise a sunflower-growing bonanza by getting the children to plant their own sunflower seeds in the outdoor area. See whose sunflower grows the quickest and tallest. Young children will soon lose interest in the growth process if nothing appears to be happening. Your enthusiasm, constant checking for new growth and exuberance when shoots appear will carry the children through this waiting period and make for an exciting learning experience. Explain that growth can often be very slow. (Slugs will love your new plants, but remember that slug pellets are dangerous if ingested.)

● Regularly share stories and information books about the life cycles of animals and plants. A couple of good examples are *The Very Hungry Caterpillar* by Eric Carle (Puffin) and *Life as a Sunflower* by Victoria Parker (Heinemann Library, *Little Nipper* series). Draw comparisons with human life cycles by including stories such as *Minnie and her Baby Brother* by Melanie Walsh (Walker Books).

You Can... Explore maths in the environment

Almost everything in the environment lends itself to mathematical concepts of sorting and classifying by colour, function, taste, shape, pattern and so on. There are many opportunities for helping children to understand their environment as they apply these concepts. For instance, going outside and counting cars passing the school gate as part of a traffic survey will strongly motivate a young child to count. You might prefer to teach these concepts and skills inside to begin with, then gradually apply them outside, on a big scale, in a hands-on situation. Real experiences will reinforce ideas you introduce.

Thinking points

● Young children learn through movement, play and sensory experiences. Try to consider these three aspects as you plan for outdoor mathematical learning.

● See maths as fun. If you can show that you are enjoying yourself as you play while, at the same time, extending the children's mathematical understanding and vocabulary in a relaxed and natural way, the children will respond positively to this experience.

● Try not to labour incidental, spontaneous mathematical activities. Children can begin to predict what you are going to say next every time they line up or show you something they have made or discovered. How often do we hear ourselves say something like: *Look how well you have lined up. Let's see how many are here today?* or *What a beautiful stone. Is it heavy or light? What shape is it?* This is basic good practice, but be careful not to overdo it!

Tips, ideas and activities

● In the garden, field or park, ask the children to tell you how many flowers, molehills and so on they can see in the grass, or how many trees there are in your playground.

● Accept the suggestions made by all the children. Invite older children to suggest a way to find out how many there actually are. Test their strategies.

● Children enjoy mathematical learning when it has a real purpose and is built on what they understand. Use everyday activities, such as gardening, tidying-up routines or parking toy vehicles to teach and reinforce new concepts.

● Near the outdoor blackboard, draw a large chalk circle on the ground, and a line for the children to stand behind. Challenge them to throw a stick to land in the circle. Model how to make a mark beside each child's name if they are successful. Count up the number of marks to see who has the most. Remember to celebrate everyone's efforts.

● Collect stones and pebbles of different sizes and shapes. Ask the children to suggest an order from heaviest to lightest. How could they find out if they were right? Test their accuracy using a spring balance.

● Organise small groups to undertake a ten-minute litter pick using gloves or litter pickers. Count the number of items collected by each group and record this on the outdoor blackboard. Ask: *Which group collected the most litter? What kind of litter did we find most of? What shall we do with it now?*

● Cutting apples into halves and quarters to share at snack time outside provides a hands-on way of looking at some simple fractions.

You Can... **Successfully plan continuous outdoor provision**

If you truly value the importance of outdoor play, it must be well documented in your planning. Everyone who looks at or uses your planning should see evidence to show that you have considered the relevance of outdoor experiences in teaching and learning. Your continuous provision planning for the outdoors is just as important as your continuous provision planning for indoors. The outside should be a really useful tool for you and your team. All your planning should be in working, flexible documents which advance children's learning. If they do not serve this purpose, you need to ask yourself a few key questions.

Thinking points

● What is your outdoor provision like at the moment? How can it be improved?

● Think about what plans are needed to make sure that you have a high standard of continuous outdoor provision. What are the implications for teaching and learning?

● How do you currently plan outdoor activities? How do your staff plan? Is there a system?

● Encourage colleagues to suggest planning ideas to improve outdoor learning.

● Remember that while we all have to satisfy government guidelines, we also have to make sure that we keep children's needs at the centre of our thinking when we plan. It is easy to become overwhelmed by the paperwork and lose sight of this basic requirement.

● Does your planning help you and your team in your day-to-day running of the setting – in particular, the outdoor sessions?

Tips, ideas and activities

● Observe the children playing freely outside. Make a note of what learning is already taking place and what resources the children are using or asking for. This will help you to plan for improving outdoor learning and enhancing resources. Think about how those resources can be organised; how adults outside can help to teach and extend vocabulary and thinking.

● Use the photocopiable sheet on page 60 for long-term continuous provision for outdoor play. This will then show an overview of your objectives. Review this sheet regularly.

● Draw a plan of your outdoor area and use this as the template for your weekly planning for outdoor resources. Write the resources, and possible activities, in each area using a coloured pen.

● Ask the children to help you set up the outdoor area using this plan as a map. This is a useful strategy for encouraging those who do not choose to go outside regularly to get to know the area and see what is available to them.

You Can... Organise resources effectively

When children go outside they usually run around and explore all the possibilities before they settle down and really start to play freely. At this early stage, they might start to look for props to enhance their play. If they know what is available they are likely to access independently what they need. Outdoor resources do not need to be expensive or even specially bought. The best kind are those that can generate an open-ended imaginative response.

Thinking points

● Do the children and adults know the full range of resources that are available for outdoor play?

● How safe is the equipment you are providing for your children? Is it in good condition?

● Do the children know where the resources are kept and where they go when finished with?

● Do they know how to ask for resources which are not immediately accessible to them?

● Are children allowed to bring inside resources outside and take outside resources inside?

● Are they allowed to move resources from one part of the outdoor area to another?

● Do you have a variety of resources, and do you need to update or change any of them to continue to stimulate the children's imagination and learning?

Tips, ideas and activities

● When the children first come into your setting, show them where the resources are in each area of continuous provision outside, just as you do inside. This is important because the children need the security of knowing where things are in both environments. With this awareness, they can become confident, independent learners.

● Work with all of the adults in your setting to compile an inventory of your outdoor equipment. This knowledge will mean that everyone will be better able to contribute in meetings to planning resources for the outdoor classroom. Also, your colleagues will then be able to offer resources to enhance play as they observe and interact with the children.

● Check your outdoor equipment weekly. Broken toys can cause injury as well as disappointment.

● Label your resources clearly so that children can learn as they match and tidy away. A laminated photograph of the contents of a box works well for the pre-readers and visual learners, with a clear written label for readers.

● At the simplest level, teach the children the dialogue they will need to ask for specific resources. For example: *Please can I have...? Thank you.* Try to give them time to explain more complex requirements, such as: *I need something that will make my dinosaur talk.*

● Allow the children to move resources from one part of the outdoor area to another to develop their play theme as long as they are not interfering with other children's play.

● Encourage everyone to help you to tidy up the resources in the outdoor area when the session is finished.

● Ask the children if there are particular types of resources they would like that they do not have access to at the moment. Think about their requests and whether they are practical and reasonable.

You Can... **Plan successful observations outside**

Observations have become an integral part of our assessment and planning procedures. These observations are just as important outside as they are inside because they can tell us so much more about how a child is progressing. To be truly effective, observations need to be carefully planned and evaluated, and the outcomes used to inform future planning for the child or group observed. As well as these planned outdoor observations, it is important to continue making informal observations when outside with the children. These are not necessarily written down or recorded systematically, unless they are regarded as evidence of significant learning, but they are, nevertheless, an essential component of good observation practice.

Thinking points

● How much time can you realistically spend outside observing, where you won't be needed by the children or colleagues? Five to ten minutes is usually reasonable for a detailed observation.

● Think about why you are doing the observation. What do you want to find out? You might have concerns about a child taking inappropriate risks when climbing; maybe you want to see how well that child interacts with other children as they play outside; perhaps you want to find out if a child has understood a mathematical concept on conservation of number which you have just taught in the garden, using dinosaurs and stones…

● How will you do the observation? How will the children and adults know not to disturb you?

● Can you be sure that what you note down is a true account of what was observed and consequently an excellent tool for moving the child/group on?

Tips, ideas and activities

● Explain to the children what will happen when you or your colleagues are making an observation in the outdoor area. Tell them you will sit or stand quietly with a clipboard. Explain that you do not want to be disturbed because you are doing a very important job. Be very strict about this. Your expectation has to be that you will not be interrupted, otherwise your observation will not be as useful as it might be.

● If you are observing children in self-chosen play activities, try not to interact with them, even if they ask you questions. If you interact, you may well alter and perhaps lead the direction of play. If you do this, then the children will no longer be engaged in free play and you will no longer be an impartial observer.

● Don't make judgements as you observe. The time to do this is when the observation has finished.

● Consider how you are going to use the outcomes of these observations. Will they slot into an ongoing, formative assessment of the child? Three such observations per year, for each child, would build up a full profile of their development.

● Look at photocopiable page 62 as an example of a ten-minute outdoor observation (a blank version of this form is provided on page 61 for you to copy and use). You will see on the sheet that once the practitioner had finished the observation, she read through the notes she had made and pulled out evidence that demonstrated significant outdoor learning. She matched this to the relevant areas of learning for three- to five-year-olds. Follow this sort of technique to ensure that observation feeds into planning.

● For brief observations of spontaneous learning through play, use the blank photocopiable format on page 63.

You Can... **Plan a thorough risk assessment**

Adults in settings are often afraid of allowing children to take risks. However, children do need the opportunity to take responsible risks outside so that they can use their initiative, solve simple problems and find out what they can do by themselves. In order for them to develop an awareness of the consequences of their actions, you need to allow children sufficient time to practise, reflect and develop the skills they need to tackle outdoor challenges.

Thinking points

● Think about how your outdoor sessions are timetabled. Does the time need to be increased? For example, a 20-minute slot for the whole class can result in children having insufficient time to settle to any one activity.

● When children know they have only a short time outside they will usually rush at things and take irresponsible risks as they don't have enough time to build up the skills needed to meet the tasks.

● Is there always an adult who can help the children develop their outdoor skills? Do the children know they can always ask for help, even for the simplest task?

● Look at the clothing the children are wearing. Is it appropriate for the challenges they are setting themselves and their peers? Is it inhibiting their movement or vision?

Tips, ideas and activities

● Look at photocopiable page 55 for tips on responsible risk-taking. Keep them in mind when planning outdoor sessions.

● Before you venture outdoors, make sure all of your colleagues are clear about the boundaries regarding the children's behaviour and what sanctions they will be expected to take.

● Before you take the children outside or on a visit, it is really important that you look carefully at the area and assess the possible risks to the children. If you can do this with your whole team, so much the better.

● Look at the example of a completed risk assessment form provided on page 57. (Page 56 is a blank version of this form for you to copy and use for your own risk assessment.) The completed form is for a risk assessment of a visit to a nearby woodland. However, the same format can be used and adapted for any visit and your own outdoor space. Find out if your setting already has a standard risk assessment format that you can use.

● Agree a risk assessment format with your colleagues and seniors. Once completed, make sure it is approved and signed by them.

● When out on a trip, it is always advisable to bring a mobile phone with the setting's phone number stored, along with a list of all the emergency contact numbers for each child.

● While out on a visit, particularly in your local area, it is worth noticing features that could be changed and developing them into learning opportunities. For example, the waste recycling area for paper near the church may be an eyesore where the bins are overflowing. You could write a letter with your children to the local authority's waste management service explaining the problem. The children will begin to understand that they have a voice and can make a difference.

You Can... Plan focused activities outside

Most of the time, an adult outside will be interacting with the children at play as well as keeping an overview of what is happening in each area of provision. There are times, however, particularly with Reception and Year 1, when you will want to carry out focused activities outside. The outdoors offers many opportunities for learning across the curriculum.

Thinking points

● Young children do not separate work from play. As practitioners we need to give equal status to the learning that takes place through play, whether this is happening indoors or outdoors.

● It is important to see play as a vehicle for learning rather than a reward for learning. When a child finishes a writing task, how often have we heard ourselves say: *Well done. Now you can go and play.* Beware!

● Consider introducing a focused activity outside *after* the children have had about 45 minutes of self-chosen activities.

● How many outdoor activities do you conduct per week? Do your colleagues have any ideas for improving such focused activities?

● Think about making brief observations of significant outdoor activities. These observations can be included in the child's ongoing, formative record and in your planning. If you wish, you can use the blank format provided on photocopiable page 63 to jot down your observations.

Tips, ideas and activities

● Before conducting a focused activity outside, teach the children the skills they need to be safe, independent users of their outdoor environment. Give them time to practise and develop those skills at their own pace.

● Check that you have done a risk assessment before you run a focused activity outside. For example, check that there are no harmful bits of litter or other hazards in your outdoor area.

● Remember that focused outdoor activities can be used to extend the children's language, knowledge and understanding of the world, mathematical vocabulary and concepts, creative, imaginative and physical skills.

● Plan for another adult to be outside with you when you run a focused activity to ensure that all the children are safe and fully engaged. Alternatively, just take a small group outside by yourself. Write this point into your plan so that everyone is clear about their role.

● In your focused plan, list the bigger resources you will use outside (such as adult-size paintbrushes, buckets, watering cans and so on) to illustrate that you are making the most of outdoor play and learning opportunities.

● Plan for differentiation in your outdoor activity, just as you would inside.

● Think about how you are going to record the outcomes of your outdoor focused activity. Will you need clipboards and paper? Will you need to take photographs? Can the children speak into a dictation recorder? How will you assess these outcomes?

You Can... Plan interaction with the children (1)

It is not enough simply to provide the space and well-planned resources outside. It is important for practitioners to play with the children outside every day while at the same time monitoring their overall development – in particular, the development of gross and fine motor skills which ensure safe use of the outdoor area.
By getting involved in outdoor play with the children, you are presenting the message that it is just as important as indoor play.

Thinking points

● How often do you get involved in the children's play? Think about which outdoor sessions need to be observed and which you can play and interact in.

● Look carefully at your area to ensure there are no gaps in hedges or fences that a small child could crawl through. If these exist, they need to be included in your risk assessment, alongside an agreed action plan as to how and when this situation will be rectified.

● Think about how you can be playful and interact freely with one group of children engaged in their chosen theme while another group play by themselves. How will you manage this? Do you have extra staff to manage the various areas of the outdoor setting?

● Do you get involved in free play with all of the children?

● Remember that your involvement and interaction during play is crucial to children's overall development. Children deserve just as much attention during this type of outdoor session as they get during an indoor literacy or numeracy activity.

Tips, ideas and activities

● When you engage in play with the children, it is worth remembering that they use play as a tool to rehearse, practise and make sense of what they are learning about the world.

● Try to plan so that you can engage freely with one group while the rest of the children play safely by themselves. This can be difficult to manage but it is not impossible. Be aware that you must always have one eye on the rest of the space.

● As you interact with the children as they play outside, it is essential to remember that you are building on knowledge and experiences that they already have. This may have come from a wide range of sources, including parents and carers, grandparents, siblings, peers, television and so on. You need to value those experiences and offer a wide range of activities to make the most of them.

● As you plan, remember that when you engage in free play with the children, this should be child-led – the best learning starts with the interests of the child. Take a genuine interest in their chosen theme or topic of play and encourage it to develop rather than trying to change or suppress it.

● Regularly review your own and your staff's practice during free play. Are you sympathetic to the children's needs and ideas? Think of ways to plan equal playtime with each child in the setting.

You Can... **Create an outdoor classroom**

You Can... **Plan interaction with the children (2)**

We must give children time to get really involved in their chosen play theme. Children who are rushed will not be able to engage fully in meaningful play, and the adults will not have time to engage fully with them. A minimum of 45 minutes is ideal and gives everyone the opportunity to become absorbed. This will have implications for timetabling outdoor spaces shared by several groups, but it is a vital consideration in your planning if you are serious about the value of learning through outdoor sessions.

Thinking points

● How much do you know about how young children play? Everyone needs to reflect on their practice from time to time and update their skills. Do you need to do a little more reading? Do you need to think about your own involvement in play? Is there a course you could attend to learn more? Is there a more experienced practitioner in your setting who could advise you?

● Get excited, laugh and be playful with the children. Stop whenever a child indicates he or she has had enough. Pressure on children to complete a task when they have lost interest is unlikely to achieve any significant learning.

● Report back informally to other members of your team on your experiences of becoming really involved in play.

● Even if you are truly engaging in a child's theme, you may be rejected at some point. How will you deal with this?

Tips, ideas and activities

● In her book *Learning Through Play: Babies, Toddlers and the Foundation Years* (Hodder & Stoughton), Tina Bruce, an acknowledged expert in the field of play, describes this high level of involvement in chosen play themes as 'free-flow play'. She has devised the following list of 12 features which define this level of engagement:

1. In their play, children use the firsthand experiences that they have in life.
2. Children make up rules as they play, and keep control of their play.
3. Children make play props.
4. Children choose to play. They cannot be *made* to play.
5. Children rehearse the future in their role-playing.
6. Children pretend when they play.
7. Children play alone sometimes.
8. Children and/or adults play together, in parallel, associatively, or cooperatively in pairs or groups.
9. Each player has a personal play agenda, although they may not be aware of this.
10. Children playing will be deeply involved, and difficult to extract from their deep learning. Children at play wallow in their learning.
11. Children try out their most recent learning, skills and competencies when they play. They seem to celebrate what they know.
12. Children at play coordinate their ideas and feelings and make sense of relationships with their family, friends and culture. When play is coordinated it flows along in a sustained way. This is free-flow play.

● Use this model to help you to understand play, inside and outside. Observe the children first to make sure they satisfy at least six of the 12 features before you begin to interact. These features will indicate that the children are deeply involved in free-flow play. You can then quietly move in, playing alongside. Take your cues from the children – try not to lead or take over.

You Can... **Develop staff commitment to outdoor learning**

Outdoor learning makes a unique contribution to a child's education. At its most simple level, children can have fun as they get some exercise in the fresh air, but that is just the beginning. Your staff and colleagues need to be made aware of the importance of outdoor learning. Their support and understanding is paramount if you are to develop your setting's commitment to outdoor learning. If you treat indoor and outdoor environments with equal importance, you start from the premise that lessons learned outside complement those taught inside, and vice versa.

Thinking points
- How can you present your approach and philosophy with regard to outdoor learning to the rest of the staff in your school or setting?

- What evidence can you gather to promote the success of outdoor learning among your colleagues?

- What do your staff understand about outdoor learning and play? Are they aware of the significance? Talk to colleagues informally to find out.

- Do you know how your colleagues feel about working outside? Note their responses (positive and negative) and plan from them.

- Are there any arguments against being outdoors? Try to think of all possible solutions.

Tips, ideas and activities
- Present evidence of your own good practice of outdoor learning to all the staff in the setting. This will give a clear overview of your thinking and ideas. Relate this to current indoor practice and stress the need to give it equal importance.

- Encourage staff to think of fun activities that are practical to take outside. For example, role play, story time, painting and art, hide and seek, treasure hunt, dressing-up games, teddy bears' picnic, dancing and so on. Ask colleagues to think about how some of these activities lend themselves to the bigger space and added stimuli outside.

- Set targets that are manageable and achievable for staff. For example:
  - Each half term, each class/group will go for a walk in the park/woods.
  - Each class/group will use their timetabled slot in the outdoor area on a daily basis.
  - Each member of staff should carry out an observation of outdoor play by X date.
  - Each member of staff should have the opportunity to engage in free play by X date.

- Talk to senior colleagues and staff about the possibility of drawing up a whole-school statement or policy of commitment to outdoor learning. When making this statement, keep the children and their needs at the centre of your thinking.

- Regularly review the implementation of the statement and gradually add in more targets as colleagues, and children, become more confident in their use of the outdoors.

You Can... Involve parents and carers in outdoor learning

A highly effective way of developing your setting's commitment to outdoor play, is to encourage the support and involvement of parents and carers. Many problems in settings are caused by poor communication between members of staff, management and families. This is often because individual workloads are continuously increasing, and basic priorities, such as knowing what is happening from day to day, are overlooked. It is essential that effective communication strategies become an integral part of the setting's policy and practice. People are more likely to be receptive to new ideas if these are properly explained and there are adequate opportunities to ask questions.

Thinking points

● Think about how you can reach *all* of your parents and carers to talk about outdoor learning. A meeting would be ideal, as it would give parents the opportunity to ask questions.

● Be aware that parents and carers have personal commitments such as full- or part-time work, another child at playgroup, an elderly relative to care for and so on.

● When will it be most appropriate to hold the meeting? For example, just before your session begins, at the end of the session, in the evening to accommodate working parents?

● How can you reach those who never attend? Perhaps an informal chat as they drop off their child, with a handout explaining their role and your expectations, might be sufficient. At least you will have involved them and, more importantly, supported their child.

Tips, ideas and activities

● Think through your ideas and philosophy about your outdoor classroom. Make a list. Then look at the ideas again and put them in order of importance. Be clear in your own mind about this so that you can successfully impart your knowledge of outdoor learning to parents and carers.

● Have a box of toys available on a carpeted area for accompanying babies and very young children. If the parents and carers feel these children are welcome they are less likely to present this as an obstacle to attending this or future meetings.

● You might find it useful to follow this structure during the meeting:
  ● Give a brief summary of why it is important to play and learn outside. Talk about how children have different learning styles. Explain government guidelines relevant to why you include outdoor learning (have copies of these guidelines, setting policies and so on available for reference).
  ● Discuss *your* expectations. For example, parents/carers must provide their child with a pair of wellies with the name written inside; they need to dress their child appropriately for playing outside, whatever the weather.
  ● Talk about *their* expectations and entitlements. This can cover organisation, safety, risk assessment and so on.
  ● Provide details of the kind of learning that will be taking place through continuous provision, focused activities and adult interaction in play.
  ● Talk about the value of learning through play and how indoor and outdoor learning are of equal importance.

● For more ideas, look at *Playing Outside – Rain or Shine* by Rosaleen Joyce (Educational Printing Services).

You Can... Organise workshops for parents and carers

If you value parents and carers as the child's first educators, it is important to make this clear to them and show them how you build on the understanding the child brings to the setting. To continue the partnership and contribute to the child's learning and development, consider setting up a series of parent workshops based on the curriculum, policies regarding play, what constitutes good practice and other topics of interest or concern.

Thinking points

● Could you conduct a workshop (or series of workshops) that will demonstrate making the most of outdoor learning and play with the children? For example, maths trails in the outdoor area.

● Think about ways in which you can encourage all of the parents and carers to attend. Are there any incentives you can offer? What are the most appropriate times to hold the workshops in order to suit the majority? How many parents and carers do you want per workshop? Where exactly will the workshops be held? How long will they last? Will you need assistance from colleagues? If so, what kind of assistance?

Tips, ideas and activities

● An example of a series of three workshops on 'Observations' could look like this:

Workshop 1

● Using approved formats from your setting, show an example of a completed observation of a child playing outside. Talk about why this observation was done, what it tells us about the child and how it helps us to move the child forward in his or her learning.

● Be aware of confidentiality issues. If using an observation sheet as an example, ensure that you change the child's name on it before sharing it with other parents/carers.

Workshop 2

● Show the parents and carers how to make a simple observation of their own child at home. This allows them to see in more detail what their children are actually doing and saying when they are playing. It also gives them more confidence and insight when using their own examples for analysis at a workshop.

● Provide comprehensive handouts about good practice regarding outdoor play and its importance. Discuss the points with the parents and carers during the workshop.

Workshop 3

● Give the parents and carers a tour of your setting's outdoor area and encourage their suggestions regarding improvements. Show them the resources that the children have access to outdoors.

● Share some of the observations done at home. What can be learned from them? Include them in the child's formative assessment.

● Always ask parents and carers to fill in an evaluation sheet at the end of your workshop(s). (See blank example on page 59.) The feedback will help you plan more effectively for your next series of workshops.

The story of Rama and Sita

This is a simple version of the Hindu tale from the *Ramayana*, an Indian epic poem written over 2000 years ago. It tells how the legendary hero, Prince Rama, rescues his wife, Sita, from the evil demon, Ravana. On their return from exile, Rama and Sita are greeted by their people who have lit their path to the palace with small earthenware lamps called divas. The divas signify the triumph of light over the darkness of evil.

A long time ago in India there was a prince called Rama. He was kind and good. Rama had a wife called Sita who was gentle and kind like Rama.

The wicked queen told lies about them to Rama's father. He sent them away to the forest. Rama's brother Lakshmana went with them.

They lived with the animals in the forest, where they built a house. They were happy.

One day, when Rama was out looking for food, a demon king called Ravana saw Sita and took her away across the sea to his island.

When Rama came home and couldn't find Sita anywhere, he was so sad. He asked the animals to help him to find her.

The monkeys said, "We know where she is". Rama followed them to the sea. They couldn't get across to Ravana's island, so they made a long bridge with stones.

After a long fight, Rama killed Ravana with his bow and arrow. He took Sita home.

Rama and Sita returned home and were made king and queen. Everyone lit small lights to show they were glad.

The outdoors and responsible risk taking

10 Top Tips

1. Do a thorough written risk assessment of the area.

2. Check each day for broken glass, brambles and so on.

3. Regularly check resources and discard damaged and broken equipment.

4. Agree boundaries and sanctions with the children regarding appropriate behaviour. Make sure these are simple, clear and always carried out in the interests of everyone's safety.

5. Teach the children the skills they will need to be able to explore the environment independently.

6. Allow the children sufficient time and space to explore and develop skills at their own rate. Trust them to do this. Given the time and space, they will rarely tackle challenges beyond their levels of competence.

7. Practitioners need to have a sound knowledge of child development if their expectations of them are to be realistic.

8. Practitioners need to have a sound knowledge of the importance of play so that they can interact with the children in a truly meaningful way.

9. Don't be afraid to take a few (responsible) risks yourself. Let the children lead you.

10. Remember that accidents can happen even in the best-planned environments. Ensure that you have a policy for procedures to deal with this.

Outdoor risk assessment

This sheet should be completed by the practitioner proposing to use the space and approved by the Headteacher/Manager, and the Governing Body where appropriate.

School/setting:	Class/Group:	No of pupils:
Place to be visited:	Date(s) and time(s) of visit:	
Purpose of visit:		
Details of preparatory work:	Details of follow-up work:	
Travel arrangements:		
Departure time:	Return arrival time:	
Meal arrangements:		
Name and status of all adults (eg teacher; voluntary helper):		
First Aider:		
Details of hazards/risks:		
Overall cost of visit:		
Suggested contribution if school day:	Estimated cost to school:	
Signature of visit leader:	Date:	
Authorisation by (signature):	Date:	
Notes/reminders:		

Outdoor risk assessment – responsible risk taking

School/setting: Fairweather Primary & Nursery School	Class/Group: Reception	No of pupils: 24 at each session
Place to be visited: Woodland area at the back of the school. No roads to cross.	Date(s) and time(s) of visit: Every Tuesday am and pm, whole session.	

Purpose of visit: Essential part of our planned provision for outdoor learning.

Details of preparatory work: Planning illustrates high level of adult interaction outside to ensure children are supported in developing outdoor independence. We held a meeting with parents/carers to agree aims of woodland session and discuss 'healthy snacks'. Children are made fully aware of rules of behaviour, dress and responsible risk taking.	Details of follow-up work: Children's interests and explorations are developed. Parents/carers are informed of visit outcomes through discussion, displays etc.

Travel arrangements: On foot.

Departure time: 9.20 / 1.05	Return arrival time: 11.15 / 3.00

Meal arrangements: Healthy snack brought from home and carried in rucksack. We provide carton of milk and piece of fruit.

Name and status of all adults (eg teacher; voluntary helper): A Harding – teacher; S Smith – nursery nurse; J Scherbakov – parent; R Rahman – student.

First Aider: First Aider in setting.

Details of hazards/risks: Children might: trip on muddy ground; fall off tree stump/ trunk; bump into each other; lose footing when climbing; get stung by nettles, pricked by brambles; get a splinter; slip in dog poo; fall in a puddle; get attacked by dog; eat poisonous berries; get bitten by midges, stung by bee or wasp.

Overall cost of visit: N/A

Suggested contribution if school day: N/A	Estimated cost to school: N/A
Signature of visit leader:	Date:
Authorisation by (signature):	Date:

Notes/reminders:
- Boundaries and sanctions to be clear with all adults regarding behaviour.
- Restate boundaries and sanctions for children before setting out.
- One adult to carry several changes of clothing plus emergency first aid kit.
- Teacher to carry a whistle to alert children to danger. If they hear the whistle, they stop what they are doing and walk quietly to an adult.
- Advise people who live locally via posters in shop windows or an article in the local paper, that children are now using the woods as a learning resource and ask those people who walk their dogs there to keep them on a lead and clean up after them.
- Invite the local dog warden to come on the walk and advise on how to deal with dogs off the lead.

When we are outside

THE SQUIRREL SONG
to the tune of 'Baa Baa Black Sheep'

Chorus
I'm a grey squirrel with a bushy tail.
I've got two eyes and I've got two ears.
I've got one nose and I've got one mouth.
I look for things to nibble on
When I'm in the woods.

I'm a grey squirrel with a bushy tail.
I eat little acorns from the big oak tree.
I like to climb to the highest branch.
And then I run down again as fast as
can be.

Repeat Chorus.

LISTEN TO THE BIRDS
*Say the rhyme really quietly,
almost whispering by the time
you get to the last line.*

Listen to the birds.
Listen to the birds in the trees.
They have gone to have their tea.
Eating worms and flies.
Magpies, sparrows, crows and rooks;
Robins, starlings too.
Listen to the birds.
Listen to the birds in the trees.

WHAT WILL WE SEE IN THE WOODS TODAY?
*to the tune of 'What shall we do with
the drunken sailor?' (You can substitute
'outside' for 'in the woods'.)
Sing this before you go outside to
help the children to focus on what
they might see.*

What shall we see in the woods today?
What shall we see in the woods today?
What shall we see in the woods today –
When we go out walking?

*(Child makes a suggestion and this is used
in the next verse, as below.)*
Maybe we'll see trees in the woods.
Maybe we'll see trees in the woods.
Maybe we'll see trees in the woods.
When we go out walking.

*(On return, ask the children what
they saw.)*
What did we see in the woods today?
What did we see in the woods today?
What did we see in the woods today –
When we went out walking?

*(Again use a child's suggestion and
sing as below.)*
We saw trees in the woods today.
We saw trees in the woods today.
We saw trees in the woods today.
When we went out walking.

Parents' workshop evaluation

Workshop(s) led by:_____

on the subject of: _____

Date(s) of workshops: _____

1. Did the workshop meet your expectations?
2. What was the most useful part?
3. What was the least useful?
4. How will you use what you have learned?
5. What sort of training would you like to do with us next?
6. Any other comments:

Thank you.

You Can... **Create an outdoor classroom** **59**

Planning continuous outdoor provision

Share this planning sheet with colleagues so everyone has a clear idea of your expectations of outdoor learning.

Age group/Class:	
Date last reviewed:	
1. Observed learning opportunities in child-initiated free play	
2. Additional learning opportunities	
3. Use of adults outside	
4. Resources always available	
5. Organisation of resources	
6. Experiences we hope the children will have outside	

Planning tips/examples

1. For example, manipulative skills; concepts of height, width, distance, speed, spatial relationships and position.
2. For example, enhance observed free-play with maths principles and vocabulary.
3. Note that there will always be an adult outside. Briefly describe the role – for example, interacting with the children at play; teaching a focused activity; completing observations.
4. Resources that are kept or always taken outside.
5. How the resources are made accessible to the children.
6. Some of the key experiences you hope the children will have. For example, push and pull (a trolley of blocks) with skill, coordination and safety; observe closely and talk about seasonal change.

Detailed observation

Name:	Age:	Observer:

Date and time of observation:	Context of observation:

Observation:

Evidence of significant learning:

Next steps:

Ten-minute detailed observation – example

Name: Leah Andrews	Age: 3 years 6 months (Note exact age because of developmental differences.)	Observer: Mrs Johal
Date and time of observation: 14/4/06. 9.40–9.50	Context of observation: Leah is playing outside in the garden with her friend Delima (aged 4 years 2 months).	

Observation

Leah jumps off the stile. Picks up mobile phone.

Leah: "Can you come? Don't worry, Delima. They're here. The hospital are here. I need to ring somebody." Dials a number.

Leah: "Hello. It's Leah. It's Delima's sister here. Hello. What you doin? I'm Delima's sister. Are you busy? OK. I'll ring back later."

Leah closes the phone and follows Delima. She repeats this four times and each time the person she calls is busy. Finally she says, "OK. Can you come up later?"

Leah goes to the teacher and asks, "Can we go on a woodland walk today? Can we go on a bike ride?"

Leah: "Delima. Do you know how to do a phone? You take one hand and put your finger like this and your other finger to your ear." (She demonstrates how to make a mobile phone using her fingers.)

Delima: "I don't know how to do that before."

Leah and Delima run across the garden to the fallen tree. They scramble up, climb onto the highest branch. Leah counts 5-4-3-2-1 three times, then says, "Blast off!" and Delima jumps off the tree, quickly followed by Leah.

Evidence of significant learning

CLL: Adopts and uses dialogues she has heard adults use. Speaks clearly, in simple sentences. Asks simple questions. Can explain how to mime making a phone call.

MD: Uses numbers spontaneously in play.

CD: Engages in imaginative play. Sets the play scenario. Uses one thing to represent another, with features in common, ie fingers for phone.

PD: Plays very well with Delima, taking turns and sharing.

Next steps

1. Extend Leah's counting skills by interacting with her in play and modelling counting backwards from 10. 10, 9, 8, 7.... Blast off!

2. Invite both friends to show the class how to make a mobile phone using their fingers.

3. Introduce paramedic props to the outdoor area alongside the mobile phones. This could include a paramedic uniform (or any jacket with a label on it saying 'paramedic'), a stethoscope and a pad for making notes.

A brief observation format for evidence of spontaneous learning through play

Those little observations you see and hear throughout the day as children engage in self-chosen activities can be quickly jotted down in the format below. These short observations can be 'flapped' (stuck one under the other) in the child's record.

Example:

Name: Zak White   **Date:** 22.03.06   **Time:** 10.20

Adult making observation: Pamela James (Nursery Nurse)

Child-initiated activity / directed activity: Child-initiated activity

Whole group / small group / solitary: Small group

Area where the child was observed: Outside in the book area sitting on the bench with Max.

Brief observation of significant learning through play

Name	Age		Date
Activity chosen by the child Activity led by adult	Whole group	Small group	Solitary
Observer	Area outside where child observed		

Observation notes

Curriculum links

Also available in this series:

YOU CAN Improve your children's **WRITING**
Celia Warren
FOR AGES **4-7**

ISBN 0-439-94530-5
ISBN 978-0439-94530-1

YOU CAN Improve your children's **WRITING**
Celia Warren
FOR AGES **7-11**

ISBN 0-439-94531-3
ISBN 978-0439-94531-8

YOU CAN Create an OUTDOOR classroom
Rosaleen Joyce
FOR AGES **3-7**

ISBN 0-439-94559-3
ISBN 978-0439-94559-2

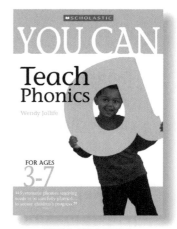

YOU CAN Teach Phonics
Wendy Jolliffe
FOR AGES **3-7**

ISBN 0-439-94554-2
ISBN 978-0439-94554-7

YOU CAN Create a CALM classroom
Sue Cowley
The best-selling author of *Getting the Buggers to Behave*
FOR AGES **4-7**

ISBN 0-439-96522-5
ISBN 978-0439-96522-4

YOU CAN Create a CALM classroom
Sue Cowley
The best-selling author of *Getting the Buggers to Behave*
FOR AGES **7-11**

ISBN 0-439-96523-3
ISBN 978-0439-96523-1

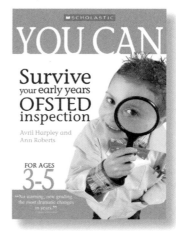

YOU CAN Survive your early years **OFSTED inspection**
Avril Harpley and Ann Roberts
FOR AGES **3-5**

ISBN 0-439-96534-9
ISBN 978-0439-96534-7

YOU CAN Use an interactive WHITE BOARD
Consultant Editor: Julie Cogill
FOR AGES **4-7**

ISBN 0-439-96539-X
ISBN 978-0439-96539-2

YOU CAN Use an interactive WHITE BOARD
Consultant Editor: Julie Cogill
FOR AGES **7-11**

ISBN 0-439-96540-3
ISBN 978-0439-96540-8

YOU CAN Create a THINKING classroom
Sue Cowley
The best-selling author of *Getting the Buggers to Behave* and *You Can Create a Calm Classroom*
FOR AGES **4-7**

ISBN 0439-96554-3
ISBN 978-0439-96554-5

YOU CAN Create a THINKING classroom
Sue Cowley
The best-selling author of *Getting the Buggers to Behave* and *You Can Create a Calm Classroom*
FOR AGES **7-11**

ISBN 0439-96555-1
ISBN 978-0439-96555-2

To find out more, call: 0845 603 9091
or visit our website www.scholastic.co.uk